23 DAYS OF TERROR
and the questions that remain . . .

- Why did authorities misidentify the sniper as a white male?

- Why were authorities so focused on a white box truck? Why did police stop John Allen Muhammad's car numerous times during October—only to let him go?

- How did the numerous law enforcement agencies and jurisdictions contribute to cracking the case?

- How did John Allen Muhammad and his alleged accomplice, Lee Boyd Malvo, act as a team? What is the nature of their relationship? And how did they obtain the arms and ammunition used?

- Did John Allen Muhammad sympathize with the 9/11 hijackers?

- What does this mean for the future of America's fight against terror?

refused. "I never saw stubbornness like that before," said her father, Marion, a thirty-year construction worker turned truck driver. Finally, all of a sudden

23

DAYS

OF TERROR

**THE COMPELLING TRUE STORY OF THE HUNT AND
CAPTURE OF THE BELTWAY SNIPERS**

ANGIE CANNON
AND THE STAFF OF *U.S. NEWS & WORLD REPORT*

POCKET BOOKS
New York   London   Toronto   Sydney   Singapore

*This book is dedicated to
the sniper victims and their families.*

An *Original* Publication of POCKET BOOKS

 POCKET BOOKS, a division of Simon & Schuster, Inc.
1230 Avenue of the Americas, New York, NY 10020

ISBN: 0-7434-7695-6

First Pocket Books printing April 2003

10 9 8 7 6 5 4 3 2 1

POCKET and colophon are registered trademarks of Simon & Schuster, Inc.

For information regarding special discounts for bulk purchases, please contact Simon & Schuster Special Sales at 1-800-456-6798 or business@simonandschuster.com

Cover design by David Griffin
Front cover photo by Manuel Ceneta-Gamma
Back cover photo by Nicholas Roberts

Printed in the U.S.A.

contents

cast of characters

LAW ENFORCEMENT

The Leaders

Charles Moose, chief of the Montgomery County Police Department

Gary Bald, special agent in charge of the FBI Baltimore field office

Michael Bouchard, special agent in charge of the Alcohol, Tobacco and Firearms Baltimore field office

Local Brass

Charles Ramsey, chief of the Washington, D.C., Metropolitan Police Department

Charlie Deane, chief of the Prince William County, Va., police department

Tom Manger, chief of the Fairfax County, Va., police department

V. Stuart Cook, sheriff of the Hanover County, Va., sheriff's department

Ronald Knight, sheriff of the Spotsylvania County, Va., sheriff's department

Gerald Wilson, chief of the Prince George's County, Md., police department

The FBI

Don Thompson, special agent in charge of the FBI's Richmond field office

George Layton, FBI supervisory special agent in Culverton, Md.

Kevin Lewis, assistant special agent in charge of the Baltimore field office

The ATF

Joe Riehl, Bouchard's top deputy in Baltimore

Walt Dandridge, firearms examiner who reviewed all ballistics evidence

Tim Curtis, Dandridge's supervisor, who reviewed his work

Jim Cavanaugh, special agent in charge in Nashville, Bouchard's No. 2

Bill McMahon, assistant special agent in charge, New York field office

Mark Chait, assistant special agent in charge, Philadelphia field office

Dan Kumor, assistant special agent in charge, Boston field office

U.S. Marshals

Billy Sorukas, supervisory inspector who worked at the headquarters of the Marshals Service

Lenny DePaul, supervisory inspector who worked in Virginia

Mike Moran, marshal who worked in the Montgomery command center

Montgomery County

Terry Ryan, homicide detective

Maryland State Police

Lt. David Reichenbaugh, operations commander
   for the criminal intelligence division

Baltimore City Police Department

Officer James Snyder, the cop who woke
   John Muhammad on October 8
Deborah Kirk, officer who listened to tapes with a
   marshal

Elected official

Doug Duncan, Montgomery County executive

THE VICTIMS IN THE OCTOBER SNIPER SHOOTINGS

The dead

James Martin, National Oceanic and Atmospheric
   Administration employee
James L. "Sonny" Buchanan Jr., landscaper
Premkumar A. Walekar, taxi driver
Sarah Ramos, housekeeper, nanny
Lori Lewis-Rivera, nanny
Pascal Charlot, carpenter
Dean Meyers, engineer
Kenneth Bridges, businessman
Linda Franklin, FBI analyst
Conrad Johnson, county bus driver

The wounded

Mother of two, shot at Spotsylvania Mall
Iran Brown, thirteen-year-old student
Jeffrey Hopper, country music singer

The sniper suspects

John Allen Muhammad, forty-one,
   a Gulf War veteran
Lee Boyd Malvo, seventeen

chronology

5:20 P.M., OCTOBER 2, 2002, window shot at Michaels craft store in Aspen Hill, Maryland. No injuries.

6:04 P.M., OCTOBER 2, James D. Martin, fifty-five, killed in the parking lot of Shoppers Food Warehouse in Wheaton, Maryland.

7:41 A.M., OCTOBER 3, James L. "Sonny" Buchanan Jr., thirty-nine, killed while pushing a lawnmower in Rockville, Maryland.

8:12 A.M., OCTOBER 3, Premkumar A. Walekar, fifty-four, killed at a Mobil station in Aspen Hill, Maryland.

8:37 A.M., OCTOBER 3, Sarah Ramos, thirty-four, killed on a bench near a retirement community in Silver Spring, Maryland.

9:58 A.M., OCTOBER 3, Lori Lewis-Rivera, twenty-five, killed while vacuuming her minivan at a Shell station, Kensington, Maryland.

9:15 P.M., OCTOBER 3, Pascal Charlot, seventy-two, killed while crossing the street at Georgia Avenue and Kalmia Road, NW, Washington, D.C.

2:30 P.M., OCTOBER 4, mother of two, forty-three, wounded in the parking lot of Michaels craft store in Spotsylvania County, Virginia.

8:09 A.M., OCTOBER 7, Iran Brown, thirteen, wounded as he arrived at middle school in Bowie, Maryland.

8:18 P.M., OCTOBER 9, Dean Harold Meyers, fifty-three, killed at the Battlefield Sunoco gas station, Manassas, Virginia.

9:30 A.M., OCTOBER 11, Kenneth Bridges, fifty-three, killed at the Four-Mile Fork Exxon gas station, Route 1, Spotsylvania County, Virginia.

9:15 P.M., OCTOBER 14, Linda Franklin, forty-seven, killed in the parking garage at Home Depot in Seven Corners Shopping Center, Fairfax County, Virginia.

7:59 P.M., OCTOBER 19, Jeffrey Hopper, thirty-seven, wounded while walking to his car from the Ponderosa in Ashland, Virginia.

5:56 A.M., OCTOBER 22, Conrad Johnson, thirty-five, killed while standing on the top step of his bus in the Aspen Hill area near Silver Spring, Maryland.

3:19 A.M., OCTOBER 24, Sniper suspects John Muhammad and Lee Malvo arrested at rest stop near Frederick, Maryland.

Prologue

Around noon on Monday, March 25, 2002, Grey-hound bus driver Jill Lynn Farrell started the three-hundred-thirty-five-mile trek from Nogales, Arizona, to Flagstaff. That was a local run, meaning lots of stops in tiny towns. There were only about five people on board. She stashed her driver's license and credit cards in a black-and-white Union Pacific pouch behind her seat.

Farrell pulled into Tucson around 1:30 P.M. A few passengers got off. A middle-aged man and a teenager climbed aboard. The driver wasn't paying much attention because she was helping a handicapped man. When she left Tucson, there still were only a handful of people on the bus. She kept heading north.

When she pulled into the Flagstaff terminal around 10:15 that night, Farrell realized that her pouch had been stolen somewhere along the line.

There were plenty of opportunities because she was getting on and off in the little towns. She canceled her credit cards right away, but forgot about one.

Farrell didn't even realize that her Visa card had been in the pouch until Bank of America notified her some weeks later that someone had used it to purchase twelve dollars and one cent's worth of gasoline on April 9 in Tacoma, Washington. The bank thought that transaction seemed fraudulent, so it closed her account.

That, Farrell thought, was the end of it.

Until Sunday, October 20.

That afternoon, she was driving a route to Flagstaff when a Greyhound customer service representative in Phoenix contacted her.

"You have to call this number," the rep said. "It's the FBI."

Farrell tensed. What did the FBI want? She rang the agent immediately.

"We have a lot of concerns about your stolen credit card," agent Mac Rominger said. "It has a connection to the sniper case."

Could he meet with her in person as soon as she got to Flagstaff, Rominger asked.

Sure, the bus driver replied.

During the rest of the drive, Farrell tried to imagine what her card had to do with the sniper case.

She pulled into the Flagstaff terminal around 10 P.M. Rominger was there waiting for her. They talked for nearly an hour.

What did she remember about the day her cards were stolen? Why had she forgotten to close that one particular card?

Farrell racked her brain. None of her passengers

from that day stuck out in her mind. The agent told her he was going to try to get her ticket list, which might show some passenger names. She mentioned the gasoline purchase in Tacoma.

The bus driver really couldn't help much more than that.

But for the more than one thousand investigators hunting the sniper, the stolen credit card would be a clue in a frustrating case with so little to go on.

Jill Farrell, however, would get sick when she learned later that her Visa account had been mentioned in a note tacked to a tree behind the Ponderosa steak house in Ashland, Virginia. A note left there after yet another shooting by the sniper terrorizing Washington, D.C. The killer had wanted police to activate the account and to deposit ten million dollars into it—a "nonnegotiable" demand to stop the killings. A note that said, "your children are not safe anywhere at any time."

In the Guard, Williams seemed to find himself. He took advanced engineering courses and learned how

1

"We Have a Problem"

Terry Ryan worked the early shift on Wednesday, October 2. It had been a glorious Indian summer day. In the suburbs of the nation's capital, the temperature nearly hit ninety degrees; the sky was clear as a bell.

Early in the evening, it was still warm, and Ryan was kicking back with a beer while his daughters finished up their Irish dancing over at the Knights of Columbus. Ryan loved the time away from the job, the time with family and friends. In a normal year, whatever that was, he and his colleagues in the Montgomery County Police Department wouldn't catch too many of the heartbreak cases that cops in the District, just across the Maryland line, did. But working homicides, Ryan had seen more than his share of tragedy. Almost always, it started with a phone call. The thought had no sooner finished rattling around in his head when Ryan's cell phone rang.

He paused, then answered it.

"We have a problem." It was a colleague, a detective from homicide.

Ryan, a forty-one-year-old strapping guy with closely cropped hair, listened intently. At 5:20 P.M., a single rifle shot had punched a nickel-size hole in the front window of a Michaels craft store in a strip mall in nearby Aspen Hill. The store wasn't crowded, and no one had been hurt. But forty-four minutes later, at 6:04 P.M., a man was shot and killed as he walked in the parking lot of the Shoppers Food Warehouse. This was in another mall, just two miles away.

Ryan's antenna went up. Days, weeks went by without a shooting. In the past year, Montgomery County had recorded just nineteen murders. "You around if we need you tonight?" the detective asked Ryan.

"Yeah, sure, if there's a problem, gimme a yell." Ryan rang off. A little while later, the girls finished their dancing. Not long after that, he helped tuck them in, all the while listening for the chirp of the cell phone, but it was silent the rest of the night. Finally, Ryan went to bed. It would be his last good night's sleep for nearly a month.

The next morning's *Washington Post* gave the shooting in the parking lot at the Shoppers Food Warehouse just five sentences on B2, in the Metro section. Another tragic shooting in a big, busy metropolis.

The shooting at Michaels didn't merit a mention.

At Montgomery County's bustling police headquarters in Rockville, Maryland, a burble of voices dominated the 6:30 A.M roll call. Everyone had a theory. Were the shootings the work of some screwball with a rifle? Teenagers messing with Dad's gun? *Do we have a problem?*

Patrol officers, detectives and higher-ups batted around competing theories. There was no consensus, except on one point: Yeah, they had a problem all right. Definitely.

Michaels is a cheery bazaar for hobbyists and semiambitious do-it-yourselfers. It sells silk flowers, wicker baskets, wreaths for almost any occasion. It's a place you'd expect to find glue guns—not rifles. Located at Northgate Plaza, a tired strip mall with other slightly down-market tenants like Dollar Place and Classic Consignment, the craft store seemed an unlikely target for a deliberate shooting of any kind. The rare customer unhappy with his purchase was cheerfully issued a refund or allowed to make an exchange. Who, in any case, would want to shoot up a craft shop?

Ann Chapman certainly had no idea. She had just finished ringing up a customer the night before, she told detectives, when she heard a sound like a large firecracker. At first, she thought it was a light bulb exploding. But then something whooshed past her ear, even pouffed her hair a bit. It blew out the light at register No. 5, sailed through a few cardboard display stands and finally lodged in the rear wall, in the framing department. When she learned it was a bullet, it took Chapman hours before she could stop shaking.

The detectives spared Chapman their conclusion: probably a missed head shot. OK, Ryan thought, but by whom? *Why?*

* * *

The Shoppers Food Warehouse is a popular discount supermarket in Wheaton, Maryland, across the county from Terry Ryan's desk at police headquarters. Open twenty-four hours a day, it's just two miles south of the Michaels store, down Georgia Avenue, a busy highway lined by endless strip malls, at the intersection with Randolph Road, another overtaxed suburban thoroughfare whose endless rush-hour traffic leaves defeated commuters leaning hopelessly on their horns.

Detectives trying to reconstruct the events of the night before focused on what appeared to be the only decent lead they had: the victim. James Martin had stopped at the Shoppers Food Warehouse to buy snacks and sodas for his son's church group and a pet elementary school mentoring program. A fifty-five-year-old program analyst for the National Oceanic and Atmospheric Administration, a family man, Martin was active in Boy Scouts and on the board of his Methodist church. In the cubicle environment around the NOAA office, where he worked on quarterly reports, agency business plans and diversity programs, Martin was known as a guy who would give you a pat on the back or tell a few jokes when the job got stressful. Martin, his colleagues said, was a guy you could count on.

Which, to those who knew him best, was not surprising. Martin had grown up in a family in rural Missouri that knew little but hard times. His father had died when he was eight, and his mother took in laundry to pay the bills. "His mother loved him dearly," said his widow, Billie Martin. "He idolized her. They didn't have a lot, but they had a lot emotionally." He worked his way through Southeast Missouri State University as a short-order cook and picking up other odd jobs. He joined the Navy and was stationed in Washington during the Vietnam War, helping families whose boys were in the jungle. Then, he went to work on Capitol Hill as a congressional aide.

Well-read, Martin was a Civil War buff and amateur genealogist who once went to the National Archives to get an ancestor's Army pay records. He was a natural storyteller who liked collecting old pictures, old books, old cans, old bottles—"the older," a friend said, "the better." He had married Billie fifteen years ago, after meeting her a few years earlier at a St. Patrick's Day gathering. He was devoted to her and to their eleven-year-old son, Ben. Quietly, he had been writing his own family's history and planned to share it with Ben someday. "He was wealthy in terms of family and friends, but very modest in terms of flaunting anything," said a friend, Larry Gaffigan. "He never thought of himself first." Said Billie Martin, "He came from a background where he was not well off, but he was well loved. It was very important to him that he, his son and I be involved in our community so we could share that with other people."

To that end, Martin had thrown himself into an office project of adopting a local school, Shepherd Elementary, in Washington, D.C., judging the science fair and arranging for the donation of ten old NOAA computers for special-education students. When the school district bureaucracy didn't move fast enough, Martin simply loaded the computers, monitors, and keyboards himself and brought them to the school in a pickup truck. "He had a sense of urgency," said Shepherd teacher LaShahn Booth. "He felt seriously that if these kids had the same technology as their suburban counterparts, the playing field would be leveled." Teachers teased Martin, saying he should have gone into teaching, but he preferred helping out quietly. "He didn't want the glory," Booth says. "This was a guy behind the scenes who was really working for the kids. Just an extremely good Samaritan. He wanted to give because he was so blessed. He was from the heart."

When Martin pulled in to the Shoppers Food Warehouse, the parking lot was jammed. After finding a space, he ambled down the sloping lot toward the store. It isn't known whether he even heard the shot that felled him. The .223-caliber slug ripped through his back, punching him forward. Security cameras caught Martin clutching his chest, but that was it.

The cops were stumped. From every perspective, Martin had been a model citizen. Devoted husband and father. Valued and dedicated employee. Reviewing the scant facts that had been pulled together overnight, Terry Ryan couldn't see it. With no crime-scene leads and no eyewitnesses, the detectives did what detectives do in such cases: look at the victim. What was it about James Martin that would cause somebody to want to put a bullet in him in a suburban shopping mall? The answer, early that Thursday morning, was nothing. Not a goddamn thing.

That morning, a number of officers were getting ready to go to the funeral of fellow cop Bill Foust, who had had a heart attack. Ryan had barely finished his first cup of coffee when he got a call from patrol supervisor Dave Anderson. It was just after 8 A.M.

"We got another one," Anderson barked.

*   *   *

The location was a Mobil station on the corner of a traffic-choked intersection, just a couple of parking lots away from Michaels.

Mechanic Warren Shifflet had been drinking a cup of coffee curbside, keeping an eye out for the inevitable fender bender in the rush-hour traffic. Alex Millhouse, another mechanic, was chatting on the pay phone in front of the station. Neither saw a thing.

The victim was Premkumar A. Walekar. A regular, he had stopped by the station that morning to fill up his taxicab. Born in Pune, India, about one hundred miles from Bombay, where he grew up, Walekar had come to the United States back in 1968, eager to go to college.

Walekar had done well, attending classes part-time at Montgomery College while working part-time at a Hot Shoppes restaurant. Shy but hardworking, Walekar eventually quit school to work full-time, taking a job driving a truck for a magazine distributor, picking up the bundles at 4 A.M. and delivering them to stores on his route. He loved to cook and worked nights as a short-order man. Every month, he sent money home to India. Once, he sent so much that his father was able to buy his own cab instead of renting one.

For all his hard work, Walekar had been richly rewarded. Years before, his brother, Vijay, had sent him a photo from India of his girlfriend's sister, Margaret. Premkumar Walekar fell in love. He came to India to meet her. He and Margaret were married two days later. Through the years, they had two children, twenty-four-year-old Andrea and twenty-three-year-old Andrew. In September, they had celebrated their twenty-sixth wedding anniversary. They had bought a house back in Pune, Walekar's hometown in India, where they planned to retire in the not-too-distant future. They had planned to move after their daughter graduated from the University of Maryland, soon to be the first in the family with an American college degree. At fifty-four, Walekar had love, family, security—all the rewards a beneficent God could bestow. So who would want to shoot him? Who would want him dead?

That morning, Walekar started his day early—something he never did. He passed Margaret at a traffic light, she on her way home from her night nursing job, he on his way to the Mobil station. They waved to each other.

At the Mobil station, Walekar bought a lottery ticket and put five dollars' worth of gas into the tank of his gray Presidential cab at pump No. 7. Suddenly, the drone of rush-hour traffic was rent by a shot.

At the pay phone, mechanic Alex Millhouse quickly told his friend, "I gotta go—someone's been hurt."

Standing at the rear of his cab, Walekar looked stunned. Blood stained his shirt and pants. He staggered a dozen feet, then gasped. "Call an ambulance," he told a woman in a minivan. Then he slumped against her van, smearing it with blood before falling to the ground. "He's been shot, he's been shot!" shouted the woman, a doctor. She started CPR.

It was no use.

Cpl. Paul Kukucka was stopped at a red light at Aspen Hill Road and Connecticut Avenue when he saw a woman running from the Mobil station, waving her arms. "This man has just been shot!" she screamed.

Kukucka pulled his squad car over, ran to Walekar lying on the pavement, and helped with chest compressions.

The time: 8:12 A.M.

After the call from Anderson, Terry Ryan pulled on his bulletproof vest. He was headed to the door when Gene Curtis, another detective, got a call. He grabbed the receiver, listened for a second, then motioned frantically for Ryan to wait. *Another one*, Curtis signaled.

Ryan's eyes blazed.

What the hell was going on?

The shooting had taken place at 7:41 A.M., thirty-one minutes before Premkumar Walekar was murdered and just five miles from the Mobil station.

The victim was James L. Buchanan Jr. Known as "Sonny" to just about everyone, the thirty-nine-year-old former landscaper had a ready grin and a big heart. He mentored kids and believed, corny as he knew others thought it sounded, that helping the less fortunate would make society a better place. A member of the regional board of the Boys and Girls Club of Greater Washington for about a decade, Buchanan regularly pitched in with holiday parties and ran the annual Christmas-tree lot, staying out in the cold all night. He gave one kid money to help him through college. "He wanted to be there for the kids," said Tim Sheahan, executive vice president of Boys and Girls Club. "He spent active time with the kids—whatever was best for the kids."

Buchanan had gotten a business degree at the University of Maryland. For years, he had run a landscaping business out of the house he shared with his

mother and a sister. More recently, he had moved to
the mountains of Virginia to help his father, a retired
Montgomery County police officer, build a dream
home near the tree farm he owned. Buchanan wasn't
married, but he had found a woman he loved.

Buchanan had gotten out of the landscape business months earlier but was doing a favor for a longtime customer, a family-run auto dealership on
Rockville Pike, one of the county's most congested
streets. He was pushing his green Lawn-Boy mower
over a narrow strip of grass behind the dealership
when there was a bang, like a piece of steel hitting the
pavement. A parking lot attendant saw Buchanan
stagger through the chain-link gate, clutching his
chest. He stumbled nearly one hundred yards before
he fell to his knees, facedown. "Someone call 911!"
the attendant yelled. Body shop manager Gary Huss
checked to see if Buchanan was breathing, then saw
blood pooling around him. Buchanan was dead on
arrival at nearby Suburban Hospital. Doctors initially
called it an "industrial accident."

A Montgomery County patrol officer at the hospital wasn't buying it. He called Detective Gene Curtis.
"You guys need to get down here," the cop said. "This
doesn't look like a lawn mower accident."

Terry Ryan was en route to the Mobil station
when his radio crackled. A motorist had reported a
suicide. Time: 8:37 A.M.

A woman sitting on a blue metal bench on International Drive near Georgia Avenue in front of a
Crisp & Juicy chicken restaurant apparently had committed suicide. Detective Jim Drewry volunteered to

check it out. He arrived minutes later and recognized the obvious: This was no suicide.

Sarah Ramos had finished a year of law school in El Salvador when she immigrated to the United States with her husband, Carlos Cruz, a professor of economics, finance, and calculus in their native country. That was two years ago. Carlos had been reluctant to move to the United States, but she convinced him that the opportunities would be greater for their seven-year-old son, Carlos Jr. Sarah wanted to make sure her son got a good education. At thirty-four, she had finally come to terms with how difficult such transitions had been. Carlos Sr. still spoke limited English. He worked part-time in a grocery, at night. Sarah hoped one day to become a lawyer, but she supported the family through baby-sitting and housekeeping jobs. They lived with her sister, but Sarah hoped her family would have their own place one day, as they had back in El Salvador. "She had plans for the future," said a niece, Rhina Villatoro. "She was always planning. She felt she needed to work hard to make them happen."

Always smiling, Sarah Ramos was a warm wife, a caring mother, and a trustworthy nanny and housecleaner for several families. "She didn't speak much English, but she was quite a presence," says Larry Gaffigan, who had employed Ramos as a housekeeper. "Kids loved her."

She was deeply religious and very involved in her Catholic church. Just two weeks earlier, she had attended a weekend retreat and come back so spiritually moved that she inspired family members to be more religious. Weeks later, her family found a poem she had written at that retreat, thanking God for her family and asking him not to abandon her husband and son. "It was as if she had a vision she would be leaving," said Gaffigan.

Wearing jeans, Sarah Ramos was sitting in her usual Thursday morning spot—the bench near the retirement community Leisure World in Silver Spring, Maryland, where her employer picked her up for work—reading a book, her purse by her side. A single high-powered bullet slammed through her head, then through the window of the Crisp & Juicy. A landscaper working nearby told police officers he saw a white box truck with black lettering drive through the parking lot, pass the victim, and head north on Georgia Avenue. There were two people inside, he said.

The cops asked more about the white box truck.

Detective Terry Ryan paced the parking lot at the Mobil station, trying to piece things together. It was a little confusing because Premkumar Walekar's body had already been removed, and officers had to rely on conflicting accounts from witnesses and paramedics. In a shirt and tie, Ryan kept looking around him. Every so often, he told a passerby, "This is not a good place to be."

2

An Ongoing Crime

Almost invariably, a police chief's arrival at a fresh crime scene can be relied on to elicit groans of despair from patrol cops and detectives. A big crime scene is usually good for one or more TV sky cams and at least one breathless on-scene account by a carefully coiffed correspondent from one of the local network affiliates. That kind of exposure is oxygen to the new breed of media-savvy police chiefs across the country.

In the heartrending days and weeks to come, when his testy, sometimes impassioned visage would dominate the television airwaves, Charles Alexander Moose would appear to be many things to many people—an enigma, an incompetent, an implacable hunter of anonymous killers. What Chief Moose definitely was not, however, in the eyes of nearly all who watched him, was a fawning, media-friendly cop-shop proprietor intent on collecting Andy Warhol's full fifteen minutes of fame. At forty-nine, Moose was the top cop in Montgomery County, the overseer of a well-trained and well-compensated force of more than one thousand patrol officers, detectives, and support personnel, responsible for protecting a population of about eight hundred ninety thousand men, women, and children in an area of carefully tended neighborhoods that covers nearly five hundred square miles.

There have been stranger marriages of man and moment, but even those who know him well say Charles Moose and Montgomery County were an odd fit. Moose never sought the chief's job there, for one thing. He had sought the top job across the District line in Washington a few years earlier and gotten the cold shoulder for his trouble, not so much as a "thanks for your interest but." Police work in general would have seemed, to the friends he confided in as a young man, a good way down the list of possibilities for Moose. Born in New York City, he was bundled south as a toddler when the family uprooted to tiny Lexington, North Carolina. In the fly-speck town, an afterthought on the way to somewhere else, educational opportunities were few. Moose attended segregated schools until the seventh grade. As late as 1975, the future chief was planning to become a criminal defense attorney because, as he later said on *Nightline Up Close*, he "didn't like the police" and was "pretty sure they made up the things they did so that they could be mean . . . to African Americans in particular."

To call Moose's journey from a North Carolina hamlet to suburban Washington, D.C., a long, strange trip would perhaps be a bit of a stretch. But not much. Law enforcement, unlike so many other areas of endeavor in American life in the twenty-first century, is still more a place of straight and narrow paths than not. Moose's path, clearly, had to be placed in the latter category. Yes, he had put in time doing the straight climb, rising from rookie patrol officer to chief of the Portland Police Bureau in an astonishing eighteen years. But he had also always insisted on charting his own path, publicly criticizing racial profiling as a technique of police work and teaching a college class in gender-conflict resolution with his wife. And quietly, steadily, he got results that mattered. On his departure from Portland, the *Oregonian* remarked on the chief's "explosive temper" and generally tempestuous stewardship of the department. But the newspaper also credited Moose with reducing the city's crime rate—a top cop's sine qua non.

As chief, first in Portland for six years, then in Montgomery County for three, there was little in Moose to suggest the star-quality possibility of klieglight chiefs like Los Angeles's Bill Bratton or New York's Ray Kelly. Moose himself doubtless would have scoffed at the notion. His friends, almost universally, agreed. Asked about the chief's most impressive qualities, they typically responded with words like stolidity, integrity, and self-confidence. Not bad traits, as it happens, for a chief of police. For the man who would be charged with leading the investigation into the killers behind the unprecedented twenty-three days of terror in and around the nation's capital, these were the qualities that, in the end, would matter most.

Which is why, when Moose's shiny cruiser pulled into the chaotic Mobil station lot not long after Premkumar Walekar's body had been removed by paramedics, there were no moans and groans among the rank and file. The chief was all business.

"What the hell's going on?" Moose asked Detective Ryan.

"We got a problem."

"What do you need?"

Ryan had been scouring the Mobil lot for clues, keeping a wary eye on the perimeter. "I wouldn't mind more people watching my back so we can do our job without constantly looking over our shoulders."

"Great idea," Moose said. "But where do you send them?"

Good question. No one knew where the shots had come from or whether the shooter was still in the area. It was as if an unseen phantom was taking the shots, then disappearing into the snarl of morning traffic.

The brass instructed Ryan and the other cops to regroup at a Home Depot parking lot nearby. They needed to assess what they had and devise a game plan. Three dead in fifty-six minutes? Plus another the night before? How the hell did that add up? They had two white men, an Indian man, and a Hispanic woman. Was it something to do with the sites? A supermarket, an auto dealership, a gas station, a bench? No rhyme or reason there either. The roads were filled with thousands of commuters, but no one saw a thing.

Go figure.

Ryan was just a minute or two from the parking lot meeting when his cell phone chirped.

"Where are you?" Sgt. Roger Thomson asked.

Ryan told him.

"Scratch it," Thomson ordered. "Get down to the Kensington Shell station. We've got another one."

That made it four bodies that morning, five in nearly sixteen hours. The time was 9:58 A.M.

Ryan reversed course, his brain racing. The first three shootings had been in directions away from the morning rush hour. Now the shooter had headed right into the thick of the maelstrom, *going the opposite way*. Ryan had been in public safety for twenty-five years, was a firefighter for a few years before becoming a cop. He got interested in law enforcement because he grew up listening to the crackle of a police scanner. His dad worked at WRC-TV, the local NBC affiliate. And even though he worked in the promotions department, he loved chasing stories and calling 'em into the newsroom. Often, his son tagged along with him. Those were the fun old days. In the years as a cop, Ryan had seen a lot of weird and awful things on the job, things that trained him to keep his emotions in check. His heart wasn't racing as he sped toward the Shell station. But he was plenty worried. The department was suddenly way beyond stretched. And what would be next? Would they try to pop a few cops? He wanted to get to the Shell station fast—and get people the hell out of there.

Lori Ann Lewis-Rivera was a beloved nanny. She was a kind, bespectacled twenty-five-year-old girl who had moved to Washington six years earlier from Mountain Home, a tiny town of ten thousand people in Idaho. Her parents saw early on that she had a fiercely stubborn streak. When she was about six, her parents ordered Lori to clean up her room. She refused. "I never saw stubbornness like that before," said her father, Marion, a thirty-year construction worker turned truck driver. Finally, all of a sudden one day, she got a garbage can and started cleaning her room out—it had taken only two years.

As a girl, Lori baby-sat, and as early as junior high school, she announced to her parents that she wanted to be a nanny someday. It was a goal she pursued seriously. When it was time for her to graduate from high school, her father told her he couldn't help her financially because money was tight. "I'll apply for a student loan," she told him. And she got one. There are only a couple of nanny schools in the country, and she looked at all of them. She studied at Northwest Nannies Institute near Portland, Oregon. "She saw this as a chance to get out of a little town," said her first employer in Washington, Ellen Weiss, a producer for National Public Radio. "I think she felt if she didn't get out, she would be stuck."

Lori was organized and determined. When Weiss met her at the airport, the new nanny literally had her suitcase in one hand and in the other, a big notebook stuffed with ideas for games, crafts and kid menus. A few weeks later, when Weiss took her to the bank to open a checking account, she insisted on getting her checks printed with the title "Professional Nanny." Said Weiss: "She was incredibly sweet and would never say no to someone. And she was headstrong in the sense that she knew what she wanted to do."

Not long after she began working for Weiss, Lori became friendly with another nanny down the street. That young woman told Lori about a Spanish-speaking Mormon church. Lori started attending with her new friend and soon converted. That's where she met Nelson Rivera, an immigrant landscaper whose childhood couldn't have been more different from her upbringing in Idaho. He was one of ten children in a family from Honduras. She spoke little Spanish, and he, little English. "It was hard to understand how they communicated with each other, but they did," said Weiss. Lewis-Rivera's father thinks they just *liked* each other instantly. Rivera was her first boyfriend, and he proposed to her on her birthday, just a few months after they met. Lori was so excited, she ran upstairs to show Weiss her ring. After their wedding, in November 1997, the couple moved in with one of Rivera's brothers. Two years after that, they were the proud parents of a little girl, Jocelin.

The morning she died, Lewis-Rivera had gone to the Shell station to vacuum out her burgundy minivan. She had bought the vehicle with help from her employer and treated it tenderly. The floor mats were out, and she had just finished the passenger side when the mechanics in the service bays heard a noise. Jimmy Akca, tinkering with a green BMW, thought an air bag had exploded. Owner John Mistry thought the power had gone out. Maybe it was a car crash at the busy intersection. They looked out and saw traffic flowing smoothly. A group of bystanders had been sitting at a bus stop near Lewis-Rivera. Seconds later, the mechanics heard them shouting, standing at the side of the minivan. "Why are they asking for us to call 911?" Akca wondered. Then he saw Lewis-Rivera lying on the ground.

By the time Terry Ryan got there, her body was gone, and all he had were sketchy accounts from "ear witnesses," cop talk for the crying bystanders who had heard something, but seen nothing. It wasn't much of a crime scene. Officers pulled videotape from the fire station across the street, but it wouldn't yield anything useful. Once again, the shooter had vanished without a trace.

The county school district—the nation's eighteenth largest—put its one hundred ninety-one public schools on Code Blue. Dozens of private schools followed suit. Exterior doors were locked; students were prohibited from going outside. Recess, field trips, and open lunch would be canceled.

At 10:12 A.M., Montgomery County police spokeswoman Capt. Nancy Demme appeared before reporters: "We're experiencing a crime, an ongoing crime that we have not experienced before."

3

Bedlam and White Box Trucks

With so little to work with, Chief Moose's officers had to start somewhere. So they seized on the eyewitness account of the white van or box truck leaving a shooting scene. In the days to come, detectives heard accounts of other suspicious white vehicles, step vans, panel trucks—who knew there were so many white delivery vehicles crawling along the roadways around the nation's capital? That Thursday, police issued a formal announcement, saying they were looking for a "white cargo van." This was later revised to a "white box truck" with black lettering on the side and, possibly, a damaged rear lift gate. The manufacturer was thought to be Isuzu. Or maybe Mitsubishi.

With guns drawn, law enforcement officers—from Montgomery County and neighboring counties, the Maryland State Police, the FBI, the Secret Service, and others—blanketed the roads, pulling over hundreds of small white box trucks all day. "We were dizzy by all the white box trucks going by," one cop said, "some with signs and markings, some without."

Lt. David Reichenbaugh, a twenty-one-year veteran with the Maryland State Police, dispatched a contingent of some sixty plainclothes state troopers to stake out shopping centers and gas stations around Montgomery County. No one knew if the killer was done for the day. Reichenbaugh was briefing his men before they took off, but he realized: "I don't even know what to tell them to look for." But he did realize something harrowing. "There's a guy out there with a high-powered rifle," said forty-three-year-old Reichenbaugh. "And our vests aren't capable of stopping any of these rounds."

As news of the shootings swept the county, parents flooded school phone lines. Some whisked their kids out of school. Outdoor activities at schools were canceled. In some schools, kids were hustled into rooms with window shades. Schools in nearby counties took similar measures.

Many office workers spent the day inside, ordering in lunch. Some businesses closed. Streets and sidewalks were deserted. Walking to the ATM suddenly seemed too great a risk. No one wanted to be exposed.

Between 8 A.M. and 4 P.M., the county's 911 operators fielded two thousand twenty calls—compared with six hundred eighty calls the day before.

At 11:19 A.M., Chief Moose appeared at a press conference. In less than sixteen hours, there had been five shootings in his community. He urged people to continue calling in tips and not give up on the deluged 911 center. "If there is a delayed response, we ask people to please understand, but we are there," he said. "We don't have the resources to respond to every white van, but we will make those priority decisions."

Moose also urged parents not to panic and rush to take their kids out of school. "We ask the parents, please let the day continue to unfold. We have no information that this has anything to do with schools. None of the victims has been of anything close to school age. None of the locations are close to the schools. . . . I think the schoolkids are safe."

Remain calm, he urged. "We don't need panic," he said. "We're trying to get our arms around it. . . . Please encourage people not to panic, to let us work through this, to let us process this, but let's not make a rush on our schools. Our schools are safe. Our children are safe at this point."

Moose was also clear and firm with reporters. He wouldn't take any questions. "You have the information that we have available," he said. "We're not discussing any strategies because, again, we don't know who we are dealing with, and we think that they might be certainly watching this, developing their strategy, and at this point, I don't want to do anything to compromise what my investigators are doing."

By afternoon, things had finally begun to settle down a bit. Chief Moose tried to calm his frightened community: "We're all concerned. We're all fearful. We don't know what we have at this point. . . . Nothing like this has ever happened in Montgomery County. This is a very safe community. Our homicide rate just increased twenty-five percent in one day."

He again appealed to the public to come forward with tips. "I am absolutely convinced that someone saw something. This is not some lightning bolt from the sky. Someone knows."

The noise of the evening rush hour was a given, unnoticed in a place where nearly every resident had to get from one place to another—job, school, personal and professional appointments—by car. The rush hour was at full bore, the bright sun still high in the sky, as a half-dozen detectives and a couple of top deputies from the Montgomery County State Attorney's office sat down around an outside picnic table in the back of the police headquarters. They had either been running around to crime scenes or locked inside all day, working the phones. Getting out into the air was a way to clear their heads. Besides, police headquarters was bedlam with reporters milling about. One by one, they went around the table, going over what investigators had found at the different crime scenes. They had autopsy reports, highly unusual so early in the game—the medical examiner's office had expedited the preliminary results. Bullet fragments had been recovered from some of the shootings. They were a clue. The fragments and the white box truck were the only leads worthy of the description.

The anger among the group crackled like heat lightning. The shootings were heinous, beyond imagining. Whoever was behind them had to be stopped, obviously. But how?

And the question, more ominous: When would he strike again?

At 7:01 P.M., an officer for Washington, D.C.'s Metropolitan Police Department stopped a blue 1990

Chevrolet Caprice with New Jersey plates in the 4400 block of Georgia Avenue NW. The driver gave the cop his license. It bore the name John Allen Muhammad, as did the car's registration. Everything matched, and the cop let him go on his way. Muhammad was the only person in the car.

This was the fourth time the Caprice had been checked by police since October 1, when officers in Fairfax, Virginia, not far from Washington on the other side of the Potomac River, ran the plates at 1:24 A.M.

The Caprice was like a bad penny, but one that had passed through so many different hands no one seemed to notice. On Wednesday, October 2, Montgomery County police officers requested a check on the Caprice's plates at 10:51 A.M. Was the car wanted? The driver? No alarm bells sounded.

At 7:47 P.M., less than two hours after James Martin had been shot Wednesday evening at the Shoppers Food Warehouse, a Montgomery County officer, suspicious about the Caprice, had the tags run again. Again nothing. And no trail, paper, electronic, or otherwise, that raised a red flag. Amazingly, even the FBI, with the biggest budget and some of the best law enforcement technology around, lacked the basic computer software to track multiple vehicle tag checks from one jurisdiction to another.

The Caprice, like a phantom, was thus permitted to ghost its way from place to place, no matter how many times suspicious cops stopped it to verify its ownership and provenance.

At 9:15 P.M., a half block from the Montgomery County border, a courtly septuagenarian had stepped from his red-brick row house in the District of Columbia and was walking toward the now empty traffic lanes of Georgia Avenue NW when he was felled by a single bullet.

Pascal Emile Charlot had come to the United States from Haiti in 1964 and become a leader of Washington's small but vibrant Haitian community. A tall, kindly man, the seventy-two-year-old father of five was an able carpenter who did little fix-it projects for his neighbors. "He was a nice old man in the neighborhood who liked staying busy and helping out his neighbors," said Karen Archer, who lived next door. He would keep an eye on people's homes during the day and pick up their newspapers or bring in a garbage can. He planned to help her strip a big, old wooden door in her house. She recalled a time he watched a new sidewalk being poured in front of her house. "That's not level," Charlot told her. "That will have water on it." And sure enough, it does. His favorite expression was: "Let me help you with that."

Charlot was devoted to his wife, who was afflicted with dementia. When he wasn't tending to her needs, though, he loved strolling the neighborhood. "He was all over the place," said Archer. He didn't have a car, so he walked or used public transportation. He played Lotto constantly and loved sitting on his porch in the mornings, reading his newspaper. In the summer, he worked in his garden, planted in bell peppers, beans, eggplants, and tomatoes one season.

Several witnesses who heard the shot said it appeared to have come from the 1100 block of Kalmia Road NW, across the street from where Charlot was shot. A witness told police he had seen a dark, older model, four-door Chevrolet Caprice, burgundy or brown with dark, tinted windows. Another witness described it as "an American-made, big police-looking car, square shaped and dark in color." The second witness had seen the car parked along the buildings in the 7800 block of Georgia Avenue NW. About ten minutes later, that person heard a single gunshot from the area where the car was parked. Then, that witness saw the car pull away, its lights off, traveling slowly west in the 1100 block of Kalmia Road. The first witness also saw the car traveling west on Kalmia with its lights off seconds after the shot.

At 10:14 P.M., police in Prince George's County, adjacent to Montgomery and just north of the District neighborhood in which Charlot had been shot an hour earlier, ran the New Jersey plates of a rattletrap, a 1990 blue Chevrolet Caprice. All clean. The cop let the car go on its way.

The Caprice vanished into the night.

4

Fathers and Sons

The man in the Caprice was John Allen Muhammad.

He was born John Allen Williams on December 31, 1960, in New Orleans, Louisiana, to Ernest Williams, a Pullman porter, and Myrtis Williams, a frail woman who would succumb to cancer little more than three years later. Ernest had disappeared, leaving John to be raised by a domineering grandfather whose sole instrument of discipline seems to have been a sound thrashing. Ernest Williams was not a presence in his son's life. Though years later, one of John's cousins saw a balding man with bright skin, cooking on a grill in the neighborhood. "He looked like a white man," Edward Holiday recalled. He asked his cousin, "Who *is* that guy?"

"That's my father," John Williams said casually.

Williams and four siblings grew up with their grandfather and several aunts in a neat, white wood-frame house with yellow trim in a pocket northwest of Baton Rouge called Scotlandville, on the banks of the muddy Mississippi River. It was one of the city's many insular African-American neighborhoods where money was scarce, but caring and discipline abundant. Residents lived in the shadow of oil refineries in a poor place called "The Field," so named for a four-block empty space in the center of the neighborhood, surrounded by modest homes and apartments. It was a favorite spot where everyone met to play. "We were poor, but I didn't know we were poor," said Pat McCallister-LeDuff, who grew up there. "The schools were dilapidated. We had old books. We didn't have good equipment. But there was so much love and nurturing in that neighborhood."

Sunday school was at the Greater King David Baptist Church. The rest of the week, the kids of Scotlandville shot marbles, rode bikes, and, generally, as kids do everywhere, hung out. Williams and his siblings were reared by two caring aunts, one a schoolteacher, the other who stayed home. Granddad was Guy Holiday, though no one ever called him that. He was Crop Pa to his fearful charges—Grandpa with a southern drawl. Crop Pa had had a job supervising the guards at a local reform school for boys. A small man, he was nevertheless a commanding presence. "When I was little, I thought my grandfather was actually God," said Edward Holiday, Williams's first cousin, who grew up with him across the street in that neighborhood. "When it started thundering, I thought, 'There goes my grandfather.'" At one time, there were some eleven grandchildren living in Crop Pa's home in Scotlandville.

Crop Pa insisted on rules, and woe to the grandchild who transgressed. Holiday remembered a night when Crop Pa wanted the kids home "when the street lights came on," but they were still out riding with friends on the back of a truck. "My grandfather walked in the house, and when John and his brothers got there, he whupped them," Holiday said. Kenneth Jackson, John Williams's lifelong friend, who grew up with him in Scotlandville, also remembers Crop Pa's stern rule of law. "His grandfather didn't put up with anything," said Jackson. "If John was in the wrong company, he would be on him. He didn't approve of any wrongdoing."

Crop Pa had a big garden planted in greens, tomatoes, butter beans, lima beans, and okra, and he treated it as if it were the Lord's Patch. All the grandchildren were expected to weed and harvest. It was not, in any sense of the word, a voluntary thing. "If you stayed there [in Crop Pa's home], you worked the garden," said Edward Holiday. "I used to feel sorry for John and his brothers." Sometimes, their grandfather would play cards with the kids, but they knew, as Holiday put it: "Our grandfather did not play. He meant business." Crop Pa died in 1995. He was about one hundred years old. John Williams did not attend the funeral.

To Edward Holiday, John Allen Williams was like a big brother. He was nearly four years older than Holiday, and the younger boy worshiped his older cousin. Holiday used to beg Williams to take him to The Field to go swinging because the older boy pushed him higher than anyone else. "It was like you were flying," recalled Holiday. "No one could push me like John." And when Williams would get tired, Holiday would bribe him with big, fat lunchmeat sandwiches, a rare treat for a boy who never had junk food but whose diet included lots of fresh vegetables from his grandfather's garden.

Those were great days. Williams and his younger cousin used to swipe bikes and climb through neighbors' windows to pilfer waffles. "People didn't mind," said Holiday. "They said, 'You came in my house and took my waffles from the icebox.' We were bad little kids." Sometimes, the two cousins would find an old, abandoned house and try to keep other "bad boys" out of it, provoking "little gang fights" with the other kids in Scotlandville. They would make go-carts out of two-by-fours, lawn mower wheels and old bike seats. "John," Holiday recalled, "would pull me all through the neighborhood."

In the rough and tumble of Scotlandville, through elementary and junior high school, Williams was known, oddly enough, as a peacemaker. "He would try to keep people out of trouble," said Kenneth Jackson. "He was always telling people not to get into trouble. If it looked like something was going to happen, John would be the one to keep everyone calm." Once, in junior high school, some of Williams's football player friends, including Jackson, were walking home from practice, and they stopped by his house. Some "neighborhood wannabe thugs" wanted to start something with the football players. "John talked us down," Jackson recalled. "He said, 'It's not worth it.'" Edward Holiday also remembers a young man of unusual sense and moral compass. "I was a bad person. But John did not do any of that. He was the person who kept you out of trouble. He was the person you looked up to and wanted to be like. He was a good, decent person."

Scotlandville High School, a pillar that held the community together back then, was a short walk from The Field. An all-black school when Williams was growing up, it finally was integrated in the 1970s when a small group of white teachers entered the scruffy classrooms. Williams's classmates remember him as tall, slender, a sharp dresser. He was quiet, though not terribly popular. "He wasn't a very outgoing person," said Janet Scott, the Class of '78 secretary. Said Class of '78 President Pat McCallister-LeDuff: "He was a guy who didn't say a whole lot. He didn't talk that much. He smiled and stood in the background and went along with the crowd. I don't remember ever seeing him upset or fighting." Ed Dotch played with Williams on the school's tennis team, where he remembers his teammate as a decent, competitive player who aimed to win. What Dotch does recall, perhaps significantly, given Williams's lone-wolf tendencies, was a willingness to pitch in for the good of the team. "He was helpful not only to me," Dotch said, "but also to other team members."

For Williams, college wasn't an option. Finances may have kept his ambitions in check, but in any case, Williams didn't speak of wanting to go. After he graduated from high school, in 1978, Williams signed up for trade school to learn welding. He did that for several years, but his friend Kenneth Jackson also persuaded him to join the Louisiana National Guard. Williams loved the uniform and showed up at the crack of dawn once a month for duty. "He loved it and was very dedicated," Jackson says. "He tried to do his best."

In the Guard, Williams seemed to find himself. He took advanced engineering courses and learned how to clean and fire a rifle. He served in the Guard until 1985, but left with two black marks on his record, the first signs of potential trouble in any official records. In August 1982, Williams pleaded guilty to disobeying a noncommissioned officer by failing to show up for post-police duty. He was fined one hundred dollars and demoted. In April 1983, he was fined one hundred dollars for hitting a noncommissioned officer. He was sentenced to seven days' confinement, but the sentence was suspended. Williams never spent a day in stir.

Good-looking, with an easy smile, John Williams never had any trouble attracting women. "John had different women in his life," said Ed Holiday. "He was a ladies' man." One of his girlfriends became pregnant with their child, a boy named Travis. Relatives and friends said that Williams had dated another girl, noting they were surprised when he married another neighborhood girl, Carol Kaglear, on November 23, 1981. Williams met Carol because his brother, Edward, dated Carol's younger sister. Williams thought Carol was a knockout. She thought the same of him, plus, he was sweet. They had a short courtship and moved into a snug mobile home on Scotlandville's Avenue M after they got married. A son, Lindbergh, was born on October 4, 1982.

Carol and John separated on November 5, 1985. Lindbergh was three. Carol accused John of cheating on her. "He was a man, and he liked women," she told CNN's Larry King. In court records, Carol Williams said her husband began living with Mildred Green while they were married. But, she added, in defense of her husband, he never hit her.

With his marriage in shambles, John Allen Williams was looking for structure. A day after he and Carol Williams separated, he enlisted in the army. It was also around this time that the man who had grown up in a strict Baptist home converted to Islam.

After the separation, John Williams moved to Washington State with Mildred Green in November 1985. John filed for divorce in Pierce County, Washington, on August 7, 1987. Carol Williams didn't fight it, and a judge granted the divorce in March 1988. Both parents were awarded joint custody of their son. Carol Williams would have primary physical custody of Lindbergh. John was to have "reasonable" visitation and pay one hundred fifty dollars a month in child support and two hundred sixty-five dollars a month in alimony.

In 1985, Williams opened a new chapter in his life. As a combat engineer with the 15th Engineer Battalion at Fort Lewis in Tacoma, Washington, Williams was trained as a metalworker and water-truck driver, but most of his service was as a combat engineer. What that meant, essentially, was building obstacles for crews manning the army's state-of-the-art M1A1 Abrams main battle tank to practice on, laying mine fields for infantry and armored units to learn to negotiate, and, when the need called for it, some demolition work from time to time.

On March 10, 1988, Williams married Mildred Green at Fort Lewis. The marriage took place six days after John's divorce from Carol was finalized. Mildred Green was a year older than her new husband, and some friends quickly came to the conclusion that she was the brains in the family. Mildred and John had a son, John Jr., on January 17, 1990. Soon afterward, Williams was transferred to the army's 84th Engineer Company in Germany.

A year later, Williams was at war. Not long after Saddam Hussein's tanks rolled into Kuwait, in August 1990, the 84th Engineer Company received its deployment orders for the Persian Gulf. Williams and his unit wouldn't see any actual combat, but they put in long days under sometimes grueling conditions, clearing mines and bulldozing holes in the hastily thrown up Iraqi defensive lines.

Despite the stress and difficult conditions, at first Williams made a good impression on superiors and colleagues. Sgt. Kip Berentson, now retired, served over Williams in Saudi Arabia during the war and remembers him well. "He had a million-dollar smile. He put a uniform on, and he was the sharpest-looking soldier, wide shoulders, strong as an ox, good haircut, clean shaven," said Berentson. "My impression was he was a million-dollar soldier."

First impressions, however, soon gave way to darker suspicions. Berentson soon concluded that, as much as Williams might look the part of the steady soldier, he was a ticking time bomb. Little things, Berentson said, would sometimes set Williams off. "I didn't trust the guy," Berentson said.

The little things soon, it seems, became bigger things. A couple of weeks before the ground war in Iraq began, Berentson woke up in the wee hours to find his tent on fire—with sixteen men asleep inside. Someone had tossed in an incendiary grenade. Berentson immediately suspected Williams and told the army's criminal investigators, who handcuffed Williams and removed him from the unit. Berentson said he didn't see Williams again until they got back to Germany. Williams wasn't charged; nor does his military record mention the incident. But Berentson couldn't forget it. He has kept Williams's name and dog-tag number in his wallet for eleven years. If he ever turned up dead under mysterious circumstances, Berentson explained, he wanted police to take a hard look at Williams. The man, he believed, was more than capable of murder.

John Williams returned from the war a different man. He complained that black soldiers faced discrimination throughout the army, Mildred Muhammad told the *Washington Post*, and charged that after the grenade incident, he was hog-tied, with his arms and legs behind his back. When sirens sounded to warn of a possible gas attack, Williams became enraged when no one offered him a gas mask. After learning that it had just been a drill, Williams felt embarrassed and humiliated. "When he got back, he was a very angry man," Mildred Muhammad told the newspaper. "I didn't know this man. The one I knew stayed in Saudi. He didn't want anyone to become close to him."

When Williams returned to the States, in 1992, he served with the 13th Engineer Battalion at Ford Ord, California. Aside from the sporadic instances of disciplinary problems, there is nothing particularly distinguished about Williams's army career. He earned various ribbons and medals, but army officials said most were routinely given on successful completion of a course or tour of duty. Williams qualified as both a hand grenade expert and an M-16 marksmanship expert. To earn the latter, Williams hit thirty-six out of forty targets at ranges of fifty to three hundred yards. Williams mustered out at Fort Lewis on April 26, 1994. After nine years in the army, he had attained the rank of sergeant.

John and Mildred Williams had two other children. Salena Denise was born on February 1, 1992, Taalibah Aanisah on May 1, 1993.

From 1994 to 1999, the family lived together in Wapato Estates, a well-kept, middle-class neighborhood in the south end of Tacoma, Washington. Wapato Estates offers a lake popular for swimming and fishing. It has a tidy park tended regularly by scout troops. It's the kind of place where kids are out riding bicycles and adults frequently are out strolling, an integrated neighborhood where most people get along well with one another. Located just miles from both the McChord Air Force Base and Fort Lewis, the neighborhood is home to many active-duty and retired military families.

The Williams family rented a thousand-square-foot rambler with a one-car garage at 7302 South Ainsworth Avenue. The neat white house with the peaked roof and beige trim was the smallest place on the block of large two-story homes with two-car garages and basketball hoops. For several years, Mildred's elderly mother lived with the family. John and Mildred were members of the Nation of Islam and attended a weekly study group at a now-defunct mosque in Seattle under the ministry of Milford Robinson. Mildred kept the books for a local mosque in Tacoma and served as secretary for an Islamic study group, according to court records.

Born in the United States in the 1930s, the Nation of Islam is a mixture of black nationalism and some

Islamic doctrine, but traditional Muslims have dismissed it. Over the years, the Nation of Islam has garnered its share of controversy, with members implicated in violence and instances of anti-Semitism. It has clashed repeatedly with other Muslim sects.

John Williams appears to have taken to heart the Nation of Islam's emphasis on family values. He cared for the three children he had with Mildred. For a time, the marriage seemed stable. Anthony Muhammad, a friend who worked behind the counter of the tiny, bustling Fish House Café in Tacoma, described the family this way: "From 1992 until 1999, John and Mildred and the children had a model family picture." Williams was known around Wapato Estates for greeting friends and neighbors with a crushing handshake. Lee Ann Terlaje, who lived near the Williamses' old house and whose nephew went to school with the Williamses' kids, said John was very strict with his three children. They were forbidden to play anywhere except their front yard or directly across the street at a family friend's house. Once, when one of Williams's children lost control of a basketball and it rolled into the street, John refused to let the child chase it. Instead, he sent the child into the house and retrieved the ball himself. Mildred Williams, neighbors said, usually stayed at home and "always had a veil over her face and on her head," Terlaje said. "The females were rarely outside except to check the mail and get the kids."

Beneath the picture of domestic tranquillity the Williams family presented to the world there was a dark, seething interior life. Months after he returned to the States, Mildred Muhammad told the *Washing-*

ton Post years later, John Williams wouldn't do anything but sit silently on a couch in the evenings. He insisted that everything around the house—meals served, beds made—had to be done with military precision.

Work was another story. Williams had formed a small business called "Express Car/Truck Mechanic." Its motto: "We come to your home or office." Mildred Williams kept the books. Customers were impressed by the fact that Williams wore surgical gloves while working on their cars. Here again, however, the exterior picture was misleading. Often, a car being worked on would sit in the street with a blue tarp over the engine for weeks. The business, in fact, was failing. Williams said money wasn't important. But at the same time, he wanted desperately, as Mildred told the *Post,* to be "the picture of success." The fastidious mechanic also racked up ten traffic offenses from October 1994 to March 1995 in Pierce County, Washington, including negligent driving, speeding, driving without a license and having an expired license—misdemeanors and lesser offenses.

To compensate, Williams focused on the inadequacies and weaknesses of others. "He studied everybody he was around," Mildred said in the newspaper interview. "He knew what words to use in order to get you to do what he wanted. He would study your anger and [try to see] how fast it would take you to calm down. . . . He is always thinking. His mind is never idle."

Failure tumbled upon failure. In 1995, Williams joined a martial-arts instructor named Felix Strozier to open Strozier & Muhammad Team of Champions. Strozier was to be the teacher. Williams provided the security deposit to rent the small concrete basement room. Williams promised to attract Muslims to the school, but that never happened. The business folded three years later.

Next, Williams's home life fell in. In July 1995, a nasty custody dispute broke out when Williams's son from his first marriage, Lindbergh, then twelve, went to visit his father in Tacoma. John Williams tried to keep Lindbergh there with him, charging in court papers that his ex-wife, Lindbergh's mother, Carol Williams, had abused him. An affidavit from a psychiatric nurse practitioner filed in the court records says that Lindbergh Williams said he didn't want to return to Louisiana because he had been hit numerous times by his mother and physically threatened by his uncle, John Williams's brother. Mildred Williams also filed an affidavit, saying that Lindbergh's mother didn't change his urine-soaked sheets when he wet the bed and that she didn't wash his clothes. "He had clothes in a plastic bag that needed washing," Mildred Williams wrote. "The smell was so bad, we threw them away."

Carol Williams fought back hard, charging in court papers that her ex-husband had had little contact with Lindbergh in the years since he left Baton Rouge. He had seen him once for two months in 1989, she said, then again in June 1995 when she sent Lindbergh to see his dad for summer vacation. In sworn statements, Carol Williams denied harming her son. "I have never abused, mistreated or otherwise neglected Lindbergh," she wrote. John Williams's brother, Edward, filed an accompanying affidavit, asserting that he had never physically threatened the boy. "I love my brother very much and always will, but John is wrong," Edward Williams wrote. "And I told him he is wrong for the thing he is doing and said. He haven't [sic] seen Lindbergh in six years. And he is trying to turn Lindbergh against the person who have [sic] always been there for him." Carol Williams got Lindbergh back that summer after Mildred helped persuade John to return him to Louisiana. But after that, the marriage wasn't the same.

The last shred of a normal life for Williams began unraveling in 1999. The karate school had crashed, and his auto repair business was in the tank. Williams's marriage to Mildred was foundering under suspicions of his seeing other women. Williams, in turn, wrongly accused Mildred of having an affair, she told the *Washington Post*. He told her he sometimes recorded her conversations. The tensions built, and Mildred stopped keeping the books for Express Car/ Truck and the Tacoma mosque. On September 8, 1999, the couple separated. On December 29, just days before the new year, Mildred filed for divorce. The filing took place two days before John Williams's birthday.

Things got worse. On February 11, 2000, Mildred Williams charged that her estranged husband had threatened her and went to court to seek a restraining order against him. The order was issued without difficulty. On March 3, Mildred filed more legal documents. "I've still been subjected," she wrote, "to John threatening to destroy my life." She had had her phone number changed three times within five days. A phone company representative said John had called to find out Mildred's phone number but had been unable to do so. "I am afraid of John," Mildred wrote.

"He was a demolition expert in the military. He is behaving very, very irrational. Whenever he does talk with me, he always says that he's going to destroy my life, and I hang up the phone."

On March 10, Williams was keeping his three children for a weekend visitation. "He always had access and I never discouraged the children from seeing their dad," Mildred Williams wrote in court papers. "Neither did I speak badly of him to them." On March 17, the landlord called her to say the rent had not been paid, so Mildred called Williams to tell him. Williams called the landlord to say he was no longer responsible for the rent. "I was not working at the time and had no monies except what John thought I should have, which was nothing," Mildred wrote.

On March 17, the Pierce County Superior Court issued an order prohibiting Williams from harassing, stalking or threatening his wife and children. On March 24, the children went to visit their father. Mildred called him on Sunday to see what time he would be bringing the kids home. He said he'd like to take them to school the next morning. He did take them to school on Monday, March 27, but their son and daughter Salena got sick and had to come home. Mildred asked him to pick up Salena, and he called back at 3:30 P.M. to say he had both girls and wanted to pick up John Jr. to take them clothes shopping. That would be fine, Mildred said, but she told him that they needed to be home by 5:30, in time for their grandmother's birthday party. They didn't show at 5:30. Mildred paged John continuously. He called at 7:30, and the children said they were at Kmart buying clothes. They said they would come home when they had finished there. Half an hour later, she paged him again. He called at 11:25 P.M. to say they were stuck in Seattle but were en route.

That was the last time Mildred heard from John. He cleaned out his children's bank accounts—a total of five hundred twenty-one dollars. And she found out later he had borrowed one thousand one hundred dollars from a business partner. "He left me completely penniless," she wrote. "We had heard nothing. We live moment to moment. I do not know where he is."

Mildred had no way of knowing it, but Williams had spirited the children to the Caribbean island of Antigua—though he would say later in court records that he had taken them there with her consent. He later wrote in court records that he had confronted her in February about an affair and they had had a "big blow-up discussion. . . . She wanted to be relieved of a lot of responsibility and consented to my parenting the children."

It was, once again, nonsense.

On May 16, still not knowing where her children were, Mildred Williams was hospitalized at Tacoma General Hospital, staying in Room 604, when she received a call from her estranged husband. When she said she wanted to find the children, he ended the conversation. He called Mildred's mother and threatened to kill his estranged wife. Mildred gave a vivid description of Williams to a hospital security officer: "Medium build, very muscular, clean shaven and very charming." Williams owned no weapons, Mildred said, but "has access to them" and "can make a weapon out of anything." She added that he was "skilled in hand-to-hand fighting" and had a history of wearing a military uniform with a name other than his own. Hospital security moved Mildred to Room 633. Incoming calls to her room were blocked.

On June 21, Mildred was awarded temporary custody of her three children. The court issued a temporary restraining order enjoining Williams to stay away from his estranged wife and the three kids. In October, the divorce became final. The restraining order was made permanent.

John Williams did not know it, but his children, whom he valued most in life, were already beginning to slip from his grasp.

John Williams and his three children arrived at V.C. International Airport in Antigua on March 28, 2000, on American Airlines Flight 5502 from Puerto Rico. He had Wyoming driver's license No. 451891495 under the name Thomas Allen Lee. He filled out immigration cards for his three children under false names: Fred Allen Lee, Theresa Lee and Lisa Lee. He filled out cards at the airport saying he was going to stay with Jeanette Reed of Longfords Estate, but even that was a lie.

Williams actually stayed with Janet Greer, the cousin of a Tacoma friend. Greer picked up Williams at the airport, and Antiguan authorities say he and his three children stayed with her for several weeks until she asked him to leave because she was suspicious he had kidnapped his children. Williams showed her a document purportedly giving him "authority" to travel with his children. Greer wasn't buying.

Soon afterward, he and the children moved into Charles and Euphernia Douglas's white wood house on Rose Street in the Ottos neighborhood. Keithley Nedd visited that house a lot and later told authorities he heard Williams boast that he was an expert shot who could shoot a man easily at a great distance.

The home on Rose Street was next door to the one-room Greenville Primary School, owned by principal Janet Harris. In April 2000, he enrolled the children and stopped by their classroom often, even playing in the schoolyard.

Williams was hard to miss on the mellow island because he was always rushing along the town's narrow streets, a pack over his shoulders. He traveled often to the States, telling people he was going for military training and returning with an odd assortment of goods to sell: batteries, power tools and fertilizer.

Shortly after he arrived in the town, he befriended Harris, who vouched for him in his application for an Antiguan passport, saying she had known him for eighteen months when, in actuality, Antiguan authorities said, she really had known him for just two months. Months later, she was arrested for helping Williams. Harris later told authorities that she had wanted to help him because he had been so helpful at school and had seemed so honest. She also wanted to help him because he had told her that his mother was Antiguan.

That, of course, turned out to be a lie too. Williams had snookered one of his children's teachers, Muriel Allen. In talking with her one day, he suggested they were related because of the mutual name "Allen." He asked her for her mother's name, and she told him it was Eva Ferris. In June 2000, Williams applied for an Antiguan passport and said his mother was Antiguan. He presented a Louisiana birth certificate purporting to be his and an Antiguan birth certificate of Eva Ferris, although authorities have not determined how he got Ferris's birth certificate. On his Louisiana birth certificate, the name "Ferris" was misspelled, and the typeface used for the words "Ferris" and "St. John's, Antigua" is different from that of the other words on the document. Another part of that certificate shows the signature of his real mother, Myrtis Williams. And the ages for Eva Ferris do not match up on the two birth certificates.

Getting a passport was important because as a citizen, Williams would not need a work permit and could easily get a Social Security card and apply for other benefits.

Even so, Williams was having a hard time finding employment. He applied for a job as a trainer of security guards for Special Security Services, one of Antigua's largest companies, providing security for hotels, airlines, banks and construction companies. When Williams came into the firm, he was pleasant, walked in a very straight manner, and looked every bit a soldier. He made a very good impression on owner Wilbur Purcell, who was very interested because of Williams's years with the U.S. military. "That's a big plus," Purcell said. That kind of experience, he thought, meant Williams could handle tough situations. The job he had for Williams—training security guards—would have paid about one thousand dollars a month in U.S. dollars, a tidy sum in Antigua. The two men shook hands, and Purcell asked Williams to return with his military and criminal records. A couple of weeks later, Williams stopped by the security office again and said he was working on the documents. "I'll be back," he promised.

He never returned.

Purcell saw Williams some weeks later, walking down the street, and noticed something odd about him. It was a small thing, but it made Purcell wonder if Williams was losing it: He had his long pants tucked into his socks. "I wondered if he was going nuts," Purcell said.

Unable to find a regular job, Williams turned to shady dealings. Antiguan authorities believe he sold forged U.S. travel documents as a way to support himself during the fourteen months he lived on the island. They believe he sold twenty sets of documents at about three thousand dollars a pop, mostly to Jamaicans. One of Williams's acquaintances told authorities that Williams arranged for those who bought documents to fly to the United States on the return portion of a ticket that originated in the States, making it less suspicious. He accompanied many of his "clients" to the United States as a shepherd, authorities said, and would return to Antigua with goods to sell to other clients. "His outgoing, friendly nature and his attractive physical attributes all lent to his being trusted and liked," according to a 2003 report by the Antiguan attorney general's task force investigating Williams's activities. Antiguan authorities also said that a witness told them that Williams had suggested blowing up Barclays Bank and kidnapping the prime minister. Officials said that witness's information had been corroborated.

Williams's smuggling caught up with him on March 11, 2001, when he was detained at the Antiguan airport after checking in with false travel documents in the name Dwight Russel. A suspicious check-in clerk called police. That day, Howard "Steve" Kelly had paid Williams two thousand five hundred dollars for the U.S. travel documents—in the name of Dwight Russel. Kelly had been told to wait in the men's room of Big Banana restaurant at the airport, Antiguan authorities said, until Williams checked in and obtained a boarding pass, which Williams would then slip him along with the travel documents. But Williams got caught. Kelly waited for hours in the men's room, and then he went home.

Williams, instead, spent two nights in the St. John's police station. On the morning of March 13, 2001, two officers were on duty at the police station. The station log notes that one of the officers went off duty for reasons of ill health at 11:39 A.M. A minute later, at 11:40 A.M., the other officer noted that Williams had "walked out" of the station. The Antiguan task force later called it "a suspicious sequence of events and an obvious gross lack of security."

Williams had disappeared.

The last of the unraveling happened fast.

On April 14, 2001, John Williams was detained at Miami International Airport. Immigration and Naturalization Service officers suspected him of trying to use false travel documents and trying to help two Jamaican women slip into the United States with phony documents. In the end, no charges were brought. But Williams had become a small blip in the vast computer brain of the federal law enforcement bureaucracy.

Nine days later, on April 23, Williams traveled to Tacoma. He had had the brush with the INS in Miami, and he had walked out of the St. John's police station. Now, he wanted to change his name. He petitioned the Pierce County District Court to change his name legally from John Allen Williams to John Allen Muhammad. While he was in the courthouse, he apparently made no attempt to review the pleadings in his divorce and custody cases.

On April 9, 2001, Mildred called the FBI Field Office in Baltimore, Maryland, to report the kidnapping of the children. She had waited a year to contact the authorities, Mildred said; she had been living in hiding at a battered-women's shelter under an assumed name because Muhammad had threatened to kill her. John Muhammad, Mildred said, had stayed in contact with his first wife, Carol, in Baton Rouge. Mildred had been speaking with Carol, and she was willing to help her locate Muhammad and the children.

It was possible, Mildred said, that the authorities could spring a trap on Muhammad. Lindbergh, the son Muhammad had fathered with Carol, was scheduled to graduate from high school in Baton Rouge on May 22. If Muhammad showed up for the event, they could grab him then, and he could lead them to the kids.

Muhammad didn't show.

On May 31, 2001, he left Antigua with the three children he had fathered with Mildred. The traveling party had a fifth member, however. His documents identified him as Lindbergh Williams.

His real name was Lee Malvo.

On February 18, 1985, Una James gave birth to a baby boy at Victoria Jubilee Hospital in Kingston, Jamaica. There was no father listed on the baby's birth certificate. A month later, the boy was given a name: Lee Boyd Malvo.

In 1990, Una James and Leslie Malvo, the boy's father, split up.

In January 1999, Una James traveled to find work in balmy Antigua, where she sold cold drinks from a stand outside the bus station. Young Lee Malvo stayed behind and boarded with different people while attending York Castle High School in northern Jamaica for seventh and ninth grades and Spalding High School for eighth grade. "He was a very mannerly child," said Spalding Principal Delcy Williams. The short, slight Malvo impressed teachers and students as friendly, quiet and smart. "He was quite unselfish and helped other students with their studies," said York Castle Bursar Joy Bailey. He enjoyed reciting poems and performing skits. "He was always there to cheer you up when you were feeling down," said classmate Deneane Tucker. "He was always happy, acting out cartoon characters."

But his blithe spirit masked other problems. Instability in Malvo's family, his teachers said, left the boy craving attention. In his years at York Castle, Malvo lived in five different places. On school records, Malvo wrote that his father was deceased. "His father was never in the picture," said teacher Donavan Johnson. "The man was not in touch with him."

Malvo turned to other older males for approval. Rayon Richards was two years ahead of him at York Castle. Malvo was full of energy, but there was nothing that suggested violence. He loved drawing and took his sketches to Richards for his approval—even if it meant walking in the rain. "He looked up to me as a big brother," said Richards. "He was insecure and needed approval and encouragement."

In York Castle teacher Winsome Maxwell's English classes, Malvo was a good writer who earned A's. At first, Malvo was well-groomed and doing exceptionally well. But then he starting coming to school unkempt. Eventually Maxwell took Malvo into the roomy house she shared with her parents, where he lived for six months, decorating his room with his drawings of cartoon characters. Maxwell said that Una James cried when the teacher told James that Maxwell had taken Lee in because, despite James's best efforts, the boy had not been properly cared for in the mother's absence.

Malvo sought attention and affection. "He would say, 'Miss, you didn't hug me today,' " Maxwell said. "And then, he would come to you for his hug. Anyone who reached out to him, he was all open arms to the person." Maxwell could tell that Malvo's smile belied his sadness. "His mommy was away from him," she said. "Any young boy would want to have his father around, and as far as he was concerned, his father was dead." Malvo formed an especially close relationship with Maxwell's own father. "Lee wanted a companion, a father figure," she said. "Anyone who offered him any affection, he would jump on to that."

One day, James called to say that a ticket would be waiting for Malvo at the airport so he could join her. Maxwell took him to the airport, but could tell he was torn. "He was excited about going to his mommy," she said, "but he cried because he didn't want to leave me."

At fourteen, Malvo arrived in Antigua on July 9, 1999. He and his mother lived in a two-room, white wood-frame house in a poor neighborhood in St. John's. In September 1999, Malvo enrolled in the Seventh-Day Adventist School, with his mother paying the six-hundred-dollars-a-trimester tuition.

But James, apparently trying to flee poverty, dreamed of America. She was looking for someone who could get her there. The person she found, Antiguan authorities said, was John Williams, who was running a thriving black-market business providing fake documents. James left Antigua in late 2000 or early 2001.

Malvo lived alone for about three months, and authorities believe that his mother sent money to Williams for her son and that he would visit the boy. Landlord Elmore Martin went several times to collect his one hundred twenty-five dollars' monthly rent and wasn't sure what to do: He couldn't throw out a minor. So he told Malvo he would turn off the lights. Several days later, Martin found Malvo gone and gigantic holes smashed into an interior wall "like someone had rammed their head into it." One day later, Martin stormed up to Malvo as the boy was near his school. "I can't believe you would do this," he told the boy. Malvo denied it. Stunned, Martin thought the boy had a criminal mind.

Malvo moved in with Williams and his three children on Rose Street in March 2001 and soon reportedly started calling Williams Dad.

Seventh-Day Adventist Principal Rosalind Aaron said that James used to call the school to talk to her son and to see how he was doing. Williams stopped by one day and told school officials he was the boy's uncle and guardian. Aaron was suspicious because he had such a strong American accent. She told him the school needed the mother's permission to communicate with him. But Una James called and authorized it.

Aaron noticed a change in Malvo with his mother gone. "Things were not the same," she said. "His work began to slip after his mother left." Once, the principal met with Williams to tell him about the boy's mediocre work.

"You heard what the principal said," Williams told the boy.

"Yes, sir."

During this time, Malvo began practicing Islam—a dramatic switch for a boy who had attended Seventh-Day Adventist services most of his life. When Malvo mumbled something other than the standard prayers during class, the principal called him to her office.

"I can't prevent you from thinking what you think," Aaron told him. "But this is a Seventh-Day Adventist school, and I don't want you doing other religions here."

"Yes, ma'am," he said.

One day, she took his Koran from him. "When you go home, you take it home," Principal Aaron said. "You are supposed to be Seventh-Day Adventist. What is happening to you?"

Worried, Aaron knew Malvo's mother was gone and that he had been on his own. The next time Malvo's mother called, Aaron told her, "You need to talk with him. He is talking about these funny ideas."

A week or two later, Malvo was gone from school. He did not return after the Easter break.

Once he got to the United States, Malvo reunited with his mother in Fort Myers, Florida. She had married a man in hopes of becoming a U.S. citizen. Malvo immediately bonded with his new stepfather and started calling him Dad. "I said he didn't have to do that, but he wanted to," Jeremiah Neal told the Fort Myers *News-Press*. "He wanted a man to help him do man things." Malvo attended Cypress Lake High School in Fort Myers until mid-October, where the boy impressed other students with his understanding of American history.

Yet once again, Malvo's home life was falling apart. Jeremiah Neal filed for a divorce on September 13, 2001, according to the newspaper, writing, "Rushed into, but not thought out."

Una James, Antiguan authorities said, may not have paid John Williams for her forged travel documents, and he visited her in Florida. John Muhammad, who had by this point changed his name, may have "held on to Malvo as security for his payment," Antiguan authorities said.

Whether that was the reason or whether it was his disintegrating home life, Malvo left Florida for Bellingham, Washington, in mid-October 2001.

James called her son and wired him money, then was unable to reach him. She knew he was with John Allen Muhammad. And that troubled her very much.

5

A Lucky Break

At 6:35 A.M., on Friday, October 4, Chief Charles Moose held the first of several press conferences of the day.

Moose and his detectives had worked through the previous day and into the night with ballistics specialists from the U.S. Treasury Department's Bureau of Alcohol, Tobacco and Firearms to try to learn as much as they could about whoever was behind the shootings, or at least what kind of weapon he was using. They needed answers, but what they had was questions.

Lots of questions.

In less than twenty-four hours, the shootings had sent waves of fear cascading through the sprawl of Washington's hundreds of miles of suburbs and exurbs. No one who traveled the region's vast arteries of highways and four-lane business thoroughfares was safe, it seemed, while this faceless marksman continued to stalk and kill his prey.

As of the first day, Chief Moose and his detectives were running the investigation. Federal police agencies had a reputation, often well earned, for big-footing local police departments on major criminal investigations. ATF was an exception. Confronted with tricky ballistics questions, multiple shootings, multiple victims, contaminated crime scenes, any detective worth his salt wanted the experts from ATF at his elbow to help sort through the mess. Everyone knew that what ATF brought to the dance meant there was seldom the kind of unpleasantness that tended to occur when other big federal police agencies like the FBI or the Drug Enforcement Administration entered the fray with local cops.

Examining the few clues they had to work with—recovered bullet fragments from a few bodies as well as victims' entry and exit wounds—Moose's detectives and the ATF specialists had concluded that the shots appeared to have come from "a high-speed-velocity round from an assault or hunting-type weapon." This was about the only hard information Moose had to disseminate to the throng of reporters and TV news crews that had descended on his normally quiet department this Friday morning. The chief had aides pass out handouts of all the possible firearms that fit the description of the weapon suspected in the shootings. It didn't really narrow anything down, but it was something. Perhaps distributing the list would generate a lead. A hunting rifle missing from a family gun cabinet; a gun dealer who remembered something suspicious about a recent customer—stranger things had happened. Sometimes, you got lucky.

Privately, however, investigators weren't hopeful.

Ballistics evidence from the first three shootings, including the shot into the craft-shop window, was inconclusive. But the ATF crime lab concluded that fragments recovered from the other shootings seemed to have been fired from the same weapon, although there were so many different kinds of weapons it could have been.

Moose said as much as the evidence permitted him to say, no more. "We're dealing with someone shooting from a distance," he told the reporters assembled in front of him, "someone using a high-velocity round. "[We are] ninety percent sure that it is a .223 round from a rifle, a hunting rifle, an assault rifle."

The evening newscasts and the next day's papers would all carry descriptions of the bullet suspected of having been used in the shootings. The .223 is very small and fast, traveling about three thousand feet per second. When such bullets hit human flesh, they are designed to expand and fragment. That's why the damage is so severe. The ATF experts guessed that the shots had been fired from a rifle like the Colt AR-15, the semiautomatic, civilian version of the military M-16 assault rifle, which could rip through even government-issue body armor. Such a weapon could be fired with high degrees of accuracy at a distance of two hundred yards or more by a reasonably skilled marksman.

Moose appealed for the public to use the tip line, and he began wrapping up the press conference. He knew his community was nervous, edgy. School was set to start on time. No plans had been made to close. Cops were out at schools all over the county. Even as he spoke, he knew, parents were urging their young charges to hurry it up, to finish their cereal, brush their teeth, comb their hair. Moose sought to end his remarks on a reassuring note, to lower the tension a notch or two. "We feel very comfortable," he said, "that we're going to be able to get the day off to a positive start."

Before the chief turned from the lectern, he told the reporters he would be back at 8 A.M. for an update.

Charles Moose had never formally applied for the Montgomery County chief's job. His name surfaced late during the six-month national search in 1999. Perhaps the unconventional way the outsider got the post may have been more help than hindrance as he contemplated the many daunting challenges his department confronted with the unprecedented string of shootings. For one, unlike many police chiefs faced with the complexities of a big, fast-moving investigation, he was not above asking for help, even if it did mean seeking the assistance of the dreaded federals.

At forty-five, Mike Bouchard was the special agent in charge of the Baltimore field office of the federal ATF. His experts already had been working with Chief Moose's team for the better part of a day. And on Friday, Bouchard wanted to formally offer his agency's help. He was the first top federal official on the scene, but he wouldn't be the last.

All the federal agencies—the FBI, the ATF, the U.S. marshals and the Secret Service—offered help from Day One. And before long, their ranks would swell. Specialists from the CIA would pitch in. The DEA and U.S. Customs would lend a hand. The Pentagon would even provide special surveillance aircraft to help track suspicious vehicles on the highways.

The FBI would play a key role. The Bureau, for all its well-documented computer woes and screwups, has a unique software program that it uses for managing multiple leads in complex investigations. The program is called Rapid Start; cynics, bedeviled by its limitations, have sometimes called it Rapid Stall. Limitations or not, the FBI has used Rapid Start in just about every major criminal investigation, from the bombing of the Alfred P. Murrah Federal Building in Oklahoma City to the attacks on the World Trade Center and the Pentagon. If it's not quite the ideal system, it is still light-years ahead of the capabilities of most local police departments, and FBI executives around the country had scored plenty of brownie points over the years in offering Rapid Start to their local counterparts in investigations where the Bureau had no official presence.

Rapid Start would be an obvious plus to handle the thousands of leads detectives and agents would have to pursue in the investigation of multiple sniper shootings. And Gary Bald, the special agent in charge of the FBI's Baltimore field office, authorized it immediately. "It's the only thing that's been tailor-made to this kind of task," Bald said. "It's the tool of choice."

The investigation may not have been going anywhere terribly fast at the moment. But it was sure getting bigger in a hurry.

After picking up his daughter from college in Virginia, Mike Bouchard drove to the command center Chief Moose had established the day before at the Montgomery County Police Department.

It was the ATF's help Moose needed most at the moment, and Bouchard was there to see that the chief got it. Without a better fix on the ballistics picture, there was no way to get a fix on the shooter. And unless he suddenly got sloppy and tripped himself up, the shooter could go right on picking off people in gas stations, on bus benches, wherever.

When Bouchard pulled up, the Montgomery Police Department was bedlam. Reporters were camped out in what would become a tent city, with portable toilets and wall-to-wall satellite trucks. Politicians had been passing through. Inside, the command post was a relative island of sanity. Moose's investigators and other agents had commandeered a warren of twenty-five to thirty cubicles and offices on the first floor and a conference room upstairs. Inside that room, there were three tables divided into stations, each with a phone on it. Nine or ten guys had to share those phones. Agents and officers took over every inch of free space, spreading papers everywhere. A pot of coffee was brewing in a corner, and the place was stocked with water and soda.

Bouchard's specialty was arson, not shootings. In nearly twenty-three years in law enforcement, Bouchard had worked hardly any shooting homicides. He started out as a police officer in Hamden, Connecticut, a town of about fifty-two thousand residents. He stayed there seven years, then moved to ATF, where he had climbed through the ranks steadily, for fifteen years, becoming the special agent in charge, or SAC, of the Baltimore office in April 2002.

Bouchard loves the intellectual challenge of police work. On his office wall, he keeps a reminder of a case he worked involving two motorcycle gangs, each determined to blow the other up—literally. The memento is a clock that a homicide cop made for Bouchard using photos of the grungy gang members, including one dead member after a crude, homemade bomb blew up in his face. Reconstructing an arson crime scene requires patience and resolve, two traits that would serve him well in the weeks ahead as he worked side by side with Chief Moose and his team.

With so little to go on, Bouchard knew, handling the ballistics issues right would be critical. His agency would bring everything it had to bear.

Moose and Bouchard huddled quickly, catching each other up. Earlier in the day, Bouchard's top deputy, Joe Riehl, had placed one of ATF's premier forensics labs at Moose's disposal. The lab, one of just three in the country, is staffed by firearms experts and tool-mark examiners—specialists at reading the unique markings left by specific guns on fired bullets. As luck would have it, the lab, in Rockville, Maryland, is just a mile from Moose's headquarters. For consistency, one analyst—retired D.C. cop turned ATF agent Walt Dandridge—would examine all the ballistics evidence in the sniper investigation. His supervisor, Tim Curtis, would review his work. Bouchard wanted to keep the same two sets of eyes looking at all the evidence. Curtis and several other agents also went to the shooting sites to try to determine where the shooter had stood by gauging the bullet's path—part art, part science—known as "trajectory analysis."

Any spent shell casings would be an evidentiary bonanza, but they can be difficult to find. Bouchard would have his agents call out the dogs, literally. The agency used Labrador retrievers specially trained to sniff for explosives, including gunpowder residue and spent shell casings. The dogs never eat from a bowl of dog food. Instead, using food as a reward, ATF handlers train the dogs daily to detect gunpowder residue. That's the only way they get their food—so the dogs are very proficient. The Labs would go to every shooting scene, Bouchard told Moose. Before the investigation was over, Bouchard's dog handlers would be working four dogs a shift, eight in all.

Feds with dogs—one more addition to the team.

Montgomery Detective Terry Ryan went to pay a visit to his colleagues in the nation's capital just across the county line. Pascal Charlot was the only shooting victim outside Montgomery County at this point.

Ryan wanted to know more about it. Plus, he wanted to make sure D.C. knew everything Montgomery knew.

As soon as Ryan saw the oddly configured, busy intersection where the seventy-two-year-old Haitian carpenter had been shot the night before, Ryan thought, "It's him."

Later that night, ATF experts would conclusively link the shooting of Charlot to the same gun that killed the Montgomery County victims.

Ryan was studying the intersection where Charlot was killed when he got the word: There had been another shooting.

Around 2:30 P.M., a forty-three-year-old mother of two was loading packages into her minivan outside a Michaels craft store in Spotsylvania County, Virginia. Suddenly, a bullet slammed into the lower right of her back, then came out under her left breast and lodged in the back of the minivan.

A military-style Black Hawk helicopter, piloted by a member of the FBI's Hostage Rescue Team, was on call during the shooting investigation. The chopper scrambled, and before he knew it, one of Moose's detectives was airborne down to Spotsylvania, nearly sixty-five miles away. "What are we going to do," one cop asked wonderingly, "shoot these guys with a rocket?"

Finally, a lucky break—actually, two of them.

The woman who was shot not only survived but also is expected to make a full recovery. Her identity has not been made public, and her family has asked the news media to respect her wish for privacy.

The bullet that struck her was recovered from the inside of her van and whisked to the special ATF lab in Rockville. It would take another day, but the ATF's lab experts conclusively linked it to the shootings in Montgomery County and in Washington. Some hard evidence to work with.

That was the good news.

The bad news was that the shooter or shooters hadn't confined their kill zone to a tight five-mile radius. Located off Interstate 95 near Fredericksburg, Virginia, the Spotsylvania Mall wasn't like the crowded suburban region of Montgomery County, where the first shootings happened. Although increasingly becoming congested, this generally is a quiet, rural community of about ninety-eight thousand people that typically has only one or two homicides a year, usually domestic abuse or a soured drug deal.

That changed lots of things.

For Spotsylvania County Sheriff Ronald L. Knight and his small force, the shooting at the Michaels store was another painful blow for the community. Just a few months earlier, Knight and his deputies had solved the serial abduction and killing of three girls—Sofia Silva, sixteen, Kristin Lisk, fifteen, and her sister Kati, twelve—a case that had vexed them for nearly six years.

But Knight's deputies had learned an important lesson in the confounding murder case of those three girls: Never give up. "The patience is built up in thirty years of doing this job," Knight said. "We try to be the calm in the midst of the storm. If it were helter-skelter, what would the public think?"

The long hell of that case also had given Knight's deputies a chance to work hand in glove with the FBI. They had a strong relationship. The idea of a task force with the feds was not a dreaded concept to them. At fifty-three, Don Thompson was the special agent in charge of the FBI's Richmond field office, whose territory included Spotsylvania County. His agents in the Fredericksburg office responded immediately, and Thompson resurrected the old task force. Only this time, they had to add to it. "The crush of working leads required mustering more bodies," said Thompson, a thirty-year Bureau veteran. He directed a half-dozen agents from Richmond to hit the mall.

After Thursday, they had been bracing for this. Even though the previous day's shootings seemed confined to Montgomery County and the District of Columbia, the cops and agents doubted the shooter would be limited by geographic boundaries. "It became very painfully obvious that the shooter or shooters were expanding their field of operations," Thompson said.

There was another possible lead from the Spotsylvania shooting. A witness told investigators about seeing a dark-colored, older-model Chevrolet driving away from the Spotsylvania Mall. Another witness had seen a similar car the night before, right after Pascal Charlot was shot in Washington. No one was really focused on aging Chevys, however.

Everyone was looking for white box trucks and, later, white vans.

During a press conference late in the day, Chief Moose was asked if police were chasing a ghost if the white box truck turned out to be a mistake. "I want to say that no lead is a mistake," the chief said. "We will search down all leads. . . . If it turns out to not be involved, then that is the case. But we are police officers, investigators, we chase a lot of clues all the time. That's what you pay us for. So I don't feel bad about that."

6

The Faces Keep Coming

Lt. Dave Reichenbaugh was onto a great lead.

Just forty-three, Reichenbaugh was the operations commander for the criminal intelligence division of the Maryland State Police. A member of a right-wing militia group was suspected of several robberies near where the first shootings had occurred. An informant said the militia member was angry at Washington and had talked recently about killing people.

He also drove a white van, had been trying to buy a .223-caliber rifle recently, and had some kind of strange connection to Timothy McVeigh, the antisocial former Gulf War veteran who blew up the Alfred P. Murrah Federal Building in Oklahoma City.

Reichenbaugh was pumped. "Man, this is the guy," he muttered to himself. "This is the guy."

In the midst of his musings, a man tapped Reichenbaugh on the shoulder. "Son, did you get anything to eat?"

"No, sir, I haven't had a chance, but I'll get something."

A minute later, the man returned, and handed Reichenbaugh a plate of chicken wings, pizza, macaroni salad, potato salad and a soda.

"Thanks a lot," Reichenbaugh told him.

"No, thank *you*."

Only later did Reichenbaugh learn the identity of the man with the hot food and cold drink. It was Chief Moose.

They needed more space.

Not long after Chief Moose set up the command center, the thirty-first-floor cubicles and the upstairs conference room were simply not big enough to accommodate the investigation's rapidly growing size. Early into the next week, FBI supervisory special agent George Layton and Montgomery County detective Mike Mancuso stole a few hours from the case to hunt for bigger quarters. They found the perfect place just across the street, an office building adjacent to police headquarters.

Layton, a twenty-seven-year agent, called FBI headquarters to get the money. To get that approval, he first needed to designate the shootings "major case status." That meant he needed to think of a case name. First, he came up with SNIPMUR. He called his wife, who worked at headquarters. SNIP MUR, she said out loud. No way. He added an "E," and SNIPEMUR was official.

Layton got the money—nearly half a million dollars for the leased office space and rented desks, furniture, phones, fax machines, bulletin boards, and projection screens. All the stuff was delivered in no time. They took over portions of three floors, big enough for hundreds of people to work around the clock.

Which is precisely what they proceeded to do. Layton, forty-eight, was back to putting in twenty-hour days, trying to solve the case. And within days, little handmade paper signs were dangling from strings looped from the ceiling tiles throughout the new Joint Operations Center, or JOC, as everyone called it. The signs were crude but effective: Investigative, Intelligence, Hot Leads, Rapid Start, Command.

Inside the JOC, they kept the blinds drawn at all times, even on the upper floors. There was a fear that reporters might try anything to peek inside.

The noise was constant.

But there was one quiet spot at the JOC. Officers mounted photographs of each victim on a white board on one wall. Busy investigators would come and go, but they would pause and look at the faces—a constant reminder of why they were there. No one wanted to see another face go up on the board.

But the faces kept coming.

Projected on another wall in that room was a Power-Point presentation, a running list of top leads and top suspects. Those names, however, changed swiftly and often. With each new shooting, more names fell off the list. Some were cleared with good alibis. Soon others took their place.

In investigations with so little to go on, often the best leads come in over the transom. But though the phones were constantly ringing inside the JOC, no one wanted to sit around and just wait for the right call to come in. Detectives and ATF agents began reviewing all gun purchases for rifles that used .223-caliber ammunition, focusing on hunting and target rifles. They checked arrest records for owners. That first weekend, more than fifty ATF inspectors began knocking on the doors of several hundred gun dealers in Maryland and Virginia to ask if anyone had bought .223-caliber ammunition or a rifle and had acted strangely. It was a shot in the dark—one of many during the course of the investigation—because the .223 slug is one of the most common rounds of ammunition sold. The gun dealers—some sixty in Montgomery County alone—were cooperative. They told the agents they had sold that kind of ammo, but no one noticed anything alarming. They disclosed who had bought rifles that could fire that kind of bullet, but there were some 30 different guns that fit the bill. "It was a needle in a haystack," Bouchard said, "but it's a base we had to cover."

Tips poured in. By the end of the weekend, the investigation tip line had logged roughly four thousand calls, which yielded what investigators considered to be about eight hundred good leads. More than a hundred Montgomery County police officers and fifty federal agents pursued those leads. The investigation was driven by the tip line, and one cop joked that investigators found themselves mediating a lot of nasty custody disputes. They were inundated with calls from women who urged them to check out their ex-husbands—"crazy gun nuts." A lot turned out to be just bitter divorces. But through checking out tips and gun purchases, the cops also found a lot of people who legally shouldn't have had guns and got them off the streets.

One reason investigators remained so focused on white box trucks was that they kept getting so many calls about them. Then again, it seemed to every paranoid driver on the roads in and around Washington, you couldn't drive half a mile without seeing three or four of the things.

Still, some tips got more attention than others. On Saturday morning, an Aspen Hill resident called police and said he had been trying desperately to get through to the sniper hotline. Finally, he reached an officer to share his story. He said he had been at the Mobil station on Thursday but had gotten scared and left when he heard the shot. But as he was driving away, he said, he saw a white box truck parked across wide Connecticut Avenue—beyond Premkumar Walekar's gray Presidential cab—and noticed a man walking toward the driver's door. The call suddenly placed a white box truck at a second shooting on that fateful Thursday. It clinched the notion of such a vehicle.

Investigators also spent a lot of time looking at companies with multiple white box trucks registered to them. And they also were able to work with the Department of Motor Vehicles to provide information on box trucks in a given ZIP code. Again, these were long shots, but they were shots. They also reviewed surveillance videos from the latest shooting sites, although that produced nothing useful.

Mike Bouchard was beat, and he had only been working the investigation for slightly more than twenty-four hours.

He needed backup—badly.

In just about any major investigation, there is a

plan. It sounds like something from a police management handbook—the Crisis Management Incident Response Team—but it's like a battle plan. Law enforcement agents practice putting the plan into action, rehearsing it again and again. According to the ATF plan, the local special agent in charge is the incident commander; in other words, he or she is the lead investigator for that agency. Bouchard would handle the million and one jobs associated with that. But there were plenty of other fires that would need putting out. This is where the big federal police agencies can contribute in ways that locals can only dream of. By deploying veteran agents from other parts of the country and battalions of investigators from cases not quite so pressing, the federals can put a small army of cops in the field virtually overnight.

Which is what Bouchard did. He brought in Jim Cavanaugh from Nashville as a seasoned deputy. Cavanaugh had negotiated with the Branch Davidians' David Koresh at Waco. Joe Riehl and three other battle-hardened agents descended on the JOC from different points of the compass. Bill McMahon had been at the World Trade Center when it was attacked. Mark Chait drove down from Philadelphia. Dan Kumor came in from Boston. Chait and Riehl had special crisis management experience. They got to Rockville, Maryland, Saturday morning. Bouchard called a deputy assistant director at ATF headquarters in Washington and informed the brass he needed still more help—one hundred agents and twenty-five inspectors. No problem, headquarters said. Secretaries began booking blocks of motel rooms in and around Rockville.

The cavalry was on its way.

By the end of the sniper investigation, ATF had some six hundred fifty agents converged on the Washington area. As they swarmed into town, they were divided into different groups: leads, intelligence and surveillance. Case agents were assigned, meaning they were the go-to guys who would stick with the investigation until the end.

It was all a blur. After the shooting earlier on Friday in Spotsylvania County, no one knew where the shooter would turn his high-powered scope next. So, ATF agents notified their North Carolina office to give them a heads-up in case the shooter decided to head south. In addition, the bulletin said that a thirty-three-year-old man from Rockville, Maryland, had been reported missing earlier in the week by his family and could have had access to guns. Late Friday, the North Carolina Highway Patrol broadcast the ATF bulletin, which leaked to the Raleigh *News & Observer*. Around midnight, Bouchard's cell phone started ringing nonstop. National news organizations like CNN and the Associated Press were inundating ATF headquarters with calls. All Bouchard could think about was Richard Jewell, the Atlanta security guard whose life was upended after he was wrongly accused of the 1996 Olympics bombing. Bouchard kept thinking someone was going to get hurt—the media horde was camped out at this man's house. He called thirty different news organizations that night, staying on the phone until well past five in the morning and explaining to reporters that the man never was a suspect. He gave a few reporters a lecture. "You can ruin someone's reputation," he admonished. "Don't assume he's a suspect."

Saturday, Chief Moose emphatically told reporters

that the man was not a suspect and that he had been found in Fairfax, Virginia.

End of media frenzy—for the moment.

As the weekend drew to a close and a new work-week was set to begin, Chief Moose promised parents there would be increased police visibility at the schools Monday morning with help from neighboring police departments, the Maryland State Police and the Montgomery County Park Police. But he warned there were limits to what police could do, even with all the help. "Again, it is not a promise to have a police officer visible at every school, every minute," he said. "But we will absolutely do our best."

7

"Our Children Don't Deserve This"

At his first press conference of the day Monday, October 7, Chief Moose described "a regular, normal opening of school."

Minutes later, at 8:09 A.M., the sniper struck again.

Thirteen-year-old, freckle-faced Iran Brown lay writhing on the ground outside Benjamin Tasker Middle School in Bowie, Maryland, crying frantically for his aunt.

"Aunt Tanya!"

Tanya Brown looked in her rearview mirror as she pulled away. She had just dropped Iran off.

"I've been shot," he cried.

A nurse at Children's Hospital in Washington, D.C., Brown saw that her nephew was bleeding. He managed to get into the car. As she later explained on ABC's *Primetime Live,* she dialed 911 and hit her horn as she battled rush hour traffic. With no help in sight, Brown decided to drive Iran to an urgent-care clinic nearby, the Bowie Health Center. As she drove, she watched the color drain from her nephew's face, saw him struggle to breathe.

Iran was dying. "Aunt Tanya, I love you," he said.

"You're going to be OK." Tanya Brown drove like hell.

At the clinic, Dr. Tom Lyons and a medical team stabilized Iran, but he needed more help than they could give him there. The bullet had ripped through Iran's lean body, shattering a lung, his spleen, stomach, diaphragm, pancreas, liver. He was quickly airlifted to Children's Hospital. Chief surgeon Martin Eichelberger worked on him for hours. It was touch and go. The prognosis for recovery was guarded.

So was Iran.

A lone tear spilled down Chief Moose's otherwise impassive face as he addressed the crush of reporters under more television lights than ever. "Someone is so mean-spirited that they shot a child," Moose said. "Now we're stepping over the line. Because our children don't deserve this. . . . Shooting a kid. I guess it's getting really, really personal now."

Moose wasn't the only one upset. The shooting traumatized the region. Schools went into Code Blue again, canceling all outdoor activities, local field trips and afternoon kindergarten. The next morning, as helicopters whirred overhead, parents hurriedly escorted their children directly into schools, with police cars parked nearby. Maryland's Governor Parris Glendening had more than one hundred forty state troopers working with local police from both Montgomery

County and Prince George's County, the big neighboring jurisdiction where Iran Brown was shot.

The whole thing was surreal. In the mornings, parents said good-bye to their kids with a new farewell, "Be alert today. Pay attention."

Tensions escalated when investigators found a message left for them outside Iran Brown's school: the Death card from a tarot deck, which is used in fortune-telling. The shooter had handwritten a chilling message on the card: "Dear policeman, I am God." The card, along with a spent shell casing, was found in woods about one hundred fifty yards from the school entrance. A police officer who saw the card before its existence became public said, "Oh shit. Our worst fears are confirmed."

The existence of the tarot card was first reported by WUSA-Channel 9. The *Washington Post* reported it in Wednesday's editions. Detectives feared the leak would harm their chances of developing a relationship with the shooter so they could communicate with him. "I think these nuts were amazed," one said, "at how much was getting out to the press."

Chief Moose was livid. At a press conference on Wednesday, October 9, he tore into the media. "I have not received any messages that the citizens of Montgomery County want Channel 9 or the *Washington Post* or any other media outlet to solve this case," he said. "If they do, then let me know. We will go and do other police work, and we will turn this case over to the media. And you can solve it."

Moose may have been hot enough to spit tacks, but he also wanted to use the media to send a message to the shooter that he wasn't the one who released information about the tarot card. The card had contained a warning not to divulge its existence to the press. Moose realized the importance of establishing a conversation with the shooter and felt he needed to show him he had not been the one to go against his wishes.

For a man who had shunned the glory-boy image others in his station sought so sedulously, this was no easy balancing act. Nearly fifty, Moose had established a record of solid professionalism and results-oriented police work. He also had a record of giving vent to occasional volcanic rages. At times snappish and frustrated, he also was, understandably, drained and exhausted by the investigation and, at times, as with the shooting of Iran Brown, in its emotional thrall. Occasionally, too, there was the flash of a sardonic wit. Asked about the finger-pointing by different police agencies after the tarot card was leaked, Moose offered that, "unlike some parts of the Washington metropolitan area, we don't have time to have a congressional hearing to actually find out who did it." (Moose told reporters that the investigation's leaders really had reached no conclusions about who did leak it. "One part of the team thinks the other part of the team did it," the chief said. "Another third part of the team thinks the other part of the team did it." Instead, they tightened some procedures for handling evidence and tried to move on. "We are going to forget that issue," Moose said. "And we're back to continuing with the investigation.")

What people saw on television, Moose's friend Derrick Foxworth said, was the real deal. "He has the anger, but he doesn't have a proud or boastful spirit," said Foxworth, an assistant police chief in Portland. "He has a serving spirit. A lot of people had a love-hate relationship with him. Sometimes, the guy would grind on you. But you knew he had a good heart, and you knew he cared about the community and young people. He has a good sense of what law enforcement is about—and to him, it's about service."

And clearly, through it all, the pain of the victims and their families weighed most heavily on the chief. During his press conference the day Iran Brown was shot, Moose sounded more like a pastoral counselor than a grizzled policeman. Parents had to talk to their kids, Moose implored, his voice quavering. "When those kids get home, they've got to engage them," he said. "They need to hear it from their parents. They need to hear it in a way that makes sense, let them know the parents still love them, that they're safe at home and that we're going to carry on, because that's what we do in this country."

The chief, clearly, was a man of parts, not all of them immediately knowable. In the throes of the investigation, he imparted a bit of philosophical wisdom for his shaken community: "[T]he reality," he said, "is that anxiety is not all bad. I was anxious before I got married. I was anxious before I graduated from high school. There's good anxiety. I wouldn't say this is good anxiety, but at the same hand, it does alert one's senses. It does remind us of the things we find special in life."

More federals were on the way.

On Saturday, October 5, FBI Director Robert Mueller III called Moose to tell him he had the Bureau's full support, and that whatever resources he required would be placed at his disposal. At his press conference that morning, Moose also made it clear who was in charge of the investigation. "These are local homicides. We remain the jurisdiction, the lead jurisdiction," he said. "We'll remain the jurisdiction that will be responsible for prosecution of the heinous crimes in our community."

He pointed out that the shooting at the mall in Spotsylvania County was also a local crime and that the sheriff had his deputies involved in canvassing the crime scene and trying to chart the bullet's path.

"The FBI's engaged," Moose said. "They are available, but they're not demanding or insisting or even attempting to be in charge. They're simply helping. They understand these are local cases."

In some ways, Moose was drawing a line for the FBI, but he also was telling other police departments that if they had a shooting, they would not lose control. Local police departments are fiercely territorial. The chiefs run big departments—Montgomery County has more than one thousand officers. The sheriffs in many Virginia jurisdictions wield enormous power. They know their communities look to them for safety and stability. Local law enforcement agencies tend to be wary when the feds step in—there is a fear the locals will lose control of the case and credibility within their communities.

On Monday, Gary Bald, the head of the FBI's Baltimore office, received a text message on his pager. "We've had another shooting," the message said.

Bald quickly made plans. He had flown to Minneapolis to attend the annual gathering of the International Association of Chiefs of Police. Chief Moose and his wife, Sandy, had planned to attend. (Sandy Moose had just landed when a cabbie driving her to her hotel asked about the shootings near Washington; she had the driver turn around and got the next flight back home.) The ATF's Mike Bouchard had also planned to go to Minneapolis, but because his agents would be needed immediately to assist Chief Moose, he had canceled the trip. Bald had not. His assistant special agent in charge, Kevin Lewis, was in regular touch with Moose and his deputies. He had authorized the use of the Rapid Start system, and fifty computer terminals had been delivered to the JOC and installed there. Unless something else happened with the shootings, there was no reason not to go to Minneapolis.

The shooting of thirteen-year-old Iran Brown was something else. "The whole dynamic," Bald said, "changed right then."

Now they were dealing with not just multiple shootings, but multiple jurisdictions. That was reason enough for the Bureau to jump in. But it wasn't just that. Politicians, ranking members of Congress, were calling the J. Edgar Hoover Building, clamoring for action.

Bald, a twenty-five-year veteran of the FBI, knew what he had to do. Sitting on a plane for several hours would be a waste. He needed to work the phones, put people and resources into place, deal with the heat from the pols. Then he needed to think and think hard about how he would present himself to Chief Moose. At forty-eight, Bald had come home to his native Maryland to run the Baltimore office. But he had just started working there on September 30, two days before the first shootings. He didn't know Moose, but he knew plenty of other chiefs, and he knew how jealously they guarded their investigative prerogatives, how much they resented the Bureau's long-indulged inclination for big-footing. The same is true for the other federal police agencies, too, many of whose agents complain that they wind up doing all the dirty work while the Bureau boys in their Brooks Brothers suits grab all the face time in front of the cameras.

On the flight back from Minneapolis Monday afternoon, Bald had ample time to ponder all of this and more. He had asked to meet with Moose and Bouchard the following morning, and Bald cautioned himself not to prejudge the men or the meeting. "I didn't have any strategy of ideas about how I wanted things to go," he said. "I was working up a plan on how I would like things to go."

In any event, the meeting on Tuesday morning, October 8, was anticlimactic, and brief. The chief's morning press conference was to commence shortly, and he escorted Bald, a tall, thin man, reserved even by the FBI's still-extraordinary standards of reticence, out to meet the press. Chief Moose was in the process of formally requesting assistance from Attorney General John Ashcroft and told reporters that morning: "Many of our federal partners have been on site, have been very, very active and that remains the same. Any additional resources, additional layers, all of that will unfold as the investigation continues to unfold."

The top federal guys—Gary Bald and Mike Bouchard—said Moose's clarity and confidence were critical. To stop the killing, clearly, he needed help, resources, expertise and manpower no local police department could hope to provide on its own. Moose wasn't too proud to ask for the help, or to share the media spotlight with those providing it. The investigation was so big and complicated he could use all the help federal law enforcement could provide. The ATF's Bouchard likes to use a hospital analogy. Local police departments are like trauma hospitals, he said, handling nearly every problem that walks in the door. But there are some cases that require unique resources. That's when the specialists—the feds—get the call.

At one press conference that morning, Maryland Governor Glendening spoke feelingly about the criminal doing the shootings. "We're talking about a person here who is basically a coward," the governor said. "This is not an individual here who is out there doing something strong or manly or anything of this type. This is a person who is shooting elderly men, shooting women and now shooting little children."

Bald cringed. This was, emphatically, not the way to communicate with the shooter or shooters. Chief Moose was right. They did need to use the news media to try to establish a dialogue with him. But the governor's words should certainly never have been made a part of the conversation.

After the press conference, Bald asked Moose if they could talk in his office. The FBI man closed the door and assured the chief he was not planning to hijack his investigation. But he said, "I have some concerns." Bald was conscious of how his words might go over. He told the chief he was worried about calling the sniper a "coward." And he stressed the importance of the investigators' speaking with one voice, instead of a parade going to the podium prattling about their own ideas about what to do. "I have a real problem with that," Bald said.

So did Moose.

Anything anyone did to impede the investigation of the shootings and delay the apprehension of those responsible was intolerable.

The investigators would speak as one.

And they would work that way, too.

8

No Closer Than the First Day

Around 9:15 P.M., Monday, October 7, just over thirteen hours after Iran Brown was shot, Holly Thompson and Marty Ruby were closing up the Subway sandwich shop in Baltimore's working-class Remington neighborhood when a tall, black man in shorts and a T-shirt walked in.

"We're closed for the night, hon," Thompson said.

"Oh, OK," the man replied.

Fifteen minutes later, the two young women locked the front door to the sandwich shop and were walking toward a Dumpster with some trash bags when John Allen Muhammad stepped out of the shadows.

"I'm sorry, I didn't mean to scare you," he said. "I just wanted to know if I can park here for a little while and rest."

"You're OK," Thompson said. "You didn't scare us too much."

Muhammad had been driving all night, he told the women, and he was beat. He could park for a while, Marty Ruby replied, but he shouldn't leave his car there all night. "If the cops see you, they might arrest you."

Thompson glanced at the car, a blue clunker. Inside there was some kind of blue light glowing from the passenger side. Why have a TV in a beat-up car like that? she wondered. Another look revealed that the blue light was coming from a laptop computer, not a TV. The inside of the car was a total mess, she saw, jammed with clothes and boxes. "The car literally looked like someone was living in it," Thompson said.

Muhammad was polite, "very much a gentleman," Thompson recalled. He was alone, barefoot, and looked exhausted, but not disheveled. Tired as he appeared, he stood tall. "I'm not going to say he was as straight as a toothpick," Thompson said. "But he had very correct posture" and spoke with no detectable accent. "You could tell he wasn't from Baltimore."

Muhammad asked the women if they knew where he could get a hot meal. Try the 7-Eleven around the corner, the women suggested, then walked away. Looking back, they saw Muhammad resting in his car.

Not long after midnight, Muhammad strolled across the parking lot to a Mobil station and asked the eighteen-year-old cashier, Holly Holmes—Marty Ruby's sister—whether he could get hot food there. She said no, and he walked to the 7-Eleven. When he passed by again, he bought a brownie, some chips and a Coke from her. Then he said good night and left.

About half an hour later, Baltimore Police Officer James Snyder, working his regular midnight shift in the city's Northern District, passed by. As usual, he waved to Holmes behind her cashier's stall in the Mobil station. She waved back, their signal that all was well. Snyder noticed a beat-up blue Chevrolet Caprice. It was in the Subway lot, just around the corner from the gas station.

At 3 A.M., Snyder made another circuit of the block. The Caprice was still there. Suspicious, because all of the car's windows were fogged, Snyder ran the car's New Jersey plate number through a police database. It came back clean. Snyder decided to investigate anyway.

Roused from a light sleep, Muhammad handed Snyder his Washington State driver's license. Snyder ran a check to see if Muhammad was wanted anywhere. He was. There was a shoplifting complaint from Tacoma, Washington, but it didn't turn up in Snyder's computer check. Police don't enter petty crimes in national criminal databases.

Muhammad told Snyder he was traveling from Virginia to New Jersey to see his father and had stopped to rest in the parking lot. He asked how to get back to Interstate 95, and Snyder told him. John Allen Muhammad thanked the officer. Then he drove away.

The calls never stopped coming.

Day and night, they flooded the tip line. In the Joint Operations Center next door to the Montgomery County Police Department headquarters, the din of ringing phones was constant.

Most, of course, were worthless. A few sparked stampedes. Several hours after Iran Brown was shot, someone called the Prince George's County police to say he had gotten a phone message Sunday night from a mentally disturbed friend claiming responsibility for the Montgomery County shootings. The man lived within three miles of the middle school, the caller said. He had a slew of rifles. Also, he hated the cops. There had been a witness who heard the shot at Iran Brown's school and had followed a vehicle. The officers put the man's photo into a photo array. The witness said he looked like the man he saw driving near the school.

Police set up a perimeter surveillance, and officers watched the man's house all afternoon, but he didn't leave. Finally, they decided to make an arrest that evening. Armed with a court-approved search warrant, officers swarmed through the apartment, cuffed the man, and read him his Miranda rights. Pawing through his trash, an officer found receipts that would have made it impossible for the suspect to have committed one of the early shootings. And they soon found more proof that pointed to his not being the sniper. The adrenaline level suddenly plummeted. The officers released the man without charges.

Tips came from everywhere. Some were heartbreaking: A father called in his own son; a woman thought it might be her boyfriend. A gun enthusiast whose travel route to and from his job took him from Spotsylvania County to Montgomery County was a suspect, briefly. A minister called once, convinced the sniper was his former son-in-law. A trained military sniper, the man had lost his job and owned not one but two white vans. He lived in northern Virginia, but the delivery business he used to run took him regularly to Montgomery County, and he knew the place like the back of his hand. Coincidence, coincidence, coincidence.

But every one got the juices flowing. The hours were long, the coffee nasty, and the cops missed their families. But the beat cops, detectives, federal agents and patrol officers assigned to the investigation were desperate to catch the faceless marksman with the rifle. "This nut has to be him. This is our guy," one officer recalls saying about a suspect. "If this guy so much as blows his nose, we are ready to grab the tissue and check for DNA." Some were cleared with solid alibis. Other officers would watch a hot suspect around the clock, thinking he might be the sniper. Then another shooting would be reported. Suddenly, the noise in the Joint Operations Center would ebb. The name of the suspect so hot just a few minutes before would be removed from the list.

The name of another victim would be added.

"That was like being kicked in the stomach," said Lt. David Reichenbaugh, the operations commander for the criminal intelligence division of the Maryland State Police. "It was happening twice a day. And you'd realize: My God, we are no closer to this than the day it started."

Cops, including FBI snipers, were out everywhere, staking out prime possible targets, such as gas stations and strip malls. They didn't find the sniper, but the heightened anxiety across the Washington area drew all kinds of nuts and screwballs out of the woodwork. The day after Iran Brown was shot, police got a report about a suspicious vehicle at a bus stop in Aspen Hill. That's where the shootings had started, in the strip mall with the Michaels craft shop. This time, the vehicle in question was a van. The driver was acting oddly. Officers ordered the man out of the van, and he complied but tried to explain. "I have to protect our children," he said. Inside the van, the officers found a shotgun and a .45-caliber handgun. At the man's house, they found several banned assault rifles. They locked the man up.

And they still weren't any closer to finding the sniper.

On Wednesday, October 9, someone called police about a man in Kensington, an upper-middle-class Montgomery County town well known throughout the area for its many antiques stores. The man inside had a history of erratic behavior. Officers had been watching the man's house early on, but he had been ruled out after a shooting. Now, neighbors had reported loud noises coming from the home. Officers returned to his house and approached the front door. They asked the man if he owned a rifle capable of firing .223-caliber ammunition. The man had lots of weapons in the house, it turned out. In fact, the noise neighbors heard was the man blasting away at a wall inside his home. The man's guns were seized. He was taken to a mental health facility for help.

Another bum lead.

Later the same day, someone called police in a panic, saying he saw a man with a long, black bag walking into the woods near Friendly High School in Fort Washington, in Prince George's County. Police quickly cordoned off the area. They stopped a woman in a dark blue Ford and questioned her, then let her go. Schools were notified. An FBI helicopter swooped in. Police scoured an area of several hundred acres, only to discover a team of surveyors working deep in the woods. The team carried their tripods and camera gear in long, black bags. The episode was captured live by TV news crews. Local and cable channels ran the clip throughout the day.

At police headquarters, nerves were frayed. One day, after one of Chief Moose's press conferences, a TV cameraman filmed an unknown man placing an object on the chief's podium, then walking quickly away. Was it the sniper? Investigators reviewed the tape and asked the chief, the FBI's Gary Bald, and the ATF's Mike Bouchard to check their briefing sheets to see if they had received a note. Nope. Police officers soon identified the man and asked him what he had been doing. He had left a coffee cup on the podium, the man said, and had hoped to be able to introduce himself to Chief Moose. He was a fan.

Investigators manning the nonstop phones hoped that the next call would be the one that would break the case wide open, but the volume of calls, it was clear, had suddenly become one of their biggest problems. "We have almost been put in a position," Moose explained, "where any type of shooting of any magnitude that we can't immediately dismiss as domestic or [a] backfire from a vehicle, we are responding."

A growing pot of reward money merely increased the number of calls. Maryland Governor Glendening had kicked in one hundred thousand dollars in state money. All the way across the country in Montana, an anonymous businessman had added an additional fifty thousand dollars. Within days, the pot would exceed five hundred thousand dollars, most of it donated by more than nine hundred individuals and corporations.

Fear—and the overflowing pot of reward money—meant still more calls. Within days of the shooting of Iran Brown, the sniper tip line would receive six thousand twenty-five calls. Of those, one thousand two hundred fifty would be deemed "credible" leads to be pursued immediately.

This is where the FBI's Rapid Start system came into play.

Every call that came in, whether it was from an obvious crackpot or not, was logged on a Rapid Start lead sheet, an 8½-by-11-inch sheet of paper with multiple copies. Data-entry clerks would then load the information into the FBI computers that had been delivered nearly a week before to Chief Moose's new command post. Veteran FBI agents read the lead sheets and quickly determined whether they were a high or low priority.

"It was a little bit of a triage situation," Gary Bald explained.

The problem was that tips were coming in everywhere. People were calling the FBI tip line. Calls flooded individual police agencies—Montgomery County, Prince George's County, Virginia's Spotsylvania County. Complicating things was the fact that the FBI's tip line was based in the Bureau's Washington field office, way downtown, about a mile from the Capitol. It was miles from the Joint Operations Center in Rockville, a thirty-minute drive even in light traffic. Agents scanning the Rapid Start lead sheets decided not to wait to load them into the FBI computers; instead, they faxed them directly to the JOC, where investigators devoured them. The crackpot lead sheets were also sent to the JOC, but an FBI employee drove them up in a van, usually about once a day. "It really worked fairly efficiently," Bald said. "We didn't have a whole lot of redundancy . . . [but] you don't always have a system that fits every situation."

By the end of the investigation, police and federal agents would receive more than seventy thousand calls. Using the improvised Rapid Start triage system, those would be reduced to sixteen thousand leads that investigators would be assigned to run down.

To Dave Reichenbaugh, the deluge of tips and leads was overwhelming. Somewhere, he thought, in the many police and government computer databases, there had to be some scrap of information that would lead them to the sniper.

Reichenbaugh started combing through databases. The Maryland Department of Motor Vehicles was queried for a list of all owners of white Astro vans. There were seventy-seven thousand. Investigators also asked the owners of the Michaels craft shops for names of current and past employees. Shootings had occurred at two stores. Another coincidence, or not? Investigators assembled lists of gun owners from within what they had begun calling the "hot zone"— the six ZIP codes that criminal profilers suggested might have a connection to the sniper. They found seven thousand registered owners of .223-caliber weapons in Montgomery County alone, though that likely included some deer hunters.

A special law enforcement computer program

called Case Explorer allowed Reichenbaugh and his colleagues to create a new intelligence database with thousands and thousands of records. Case Explorer matches one set of facts with another, and, sometimes, comparing apples and oranges really does work. For instance, if an investigator wanted to look at all-white-Astro-van owners within a defined geographic area, then determine which of those owners had also purchased a .223-caliber rifle, Case Explorer, assuming the data it was fed were good, could come up with a set of matches. As soon as the computer spit them out, investigators in the JOC began running background checks. Days went by, and the team in the JOC widened the search, figuring the shooter might well live beyond the "hot zone." The expanded effort resulted in one thousand one hundred forty-eight Case Explorer "hot" leads—where an individual was found in two or three databases and where there was at least one tip on that person. Everyone in the JOC wanted to jump on the hot leads.

But for all the hot leads, there were missed opportunities. John Muhammad's Chevy Caprice with the New Jersey tags had been stopped by police near the scene of Pascal Charlot's murder in Washington, D.C. A witness had seen a dark, older-model Chevrolet Caprice drive away from the scene with its lights off. The next day, an eyewitness had placed a similar vehicle at the scene of the shooting in Spotsylvania County. Baltimore Police Officer James Snyder had even run a tag and license check on Muhammad and the car, but since the misdemeanor warrants for the shoplifting charges didn't come up on the computer, he was allowed to resume his travels. In all, police officers throughout the Washington, D.C., region would check John Muhammad's New Jersey tags at least nine times during October.

Muhammad and the Caprice didn't come up in the Case Explorer searches. Muhammad had a Washington State driver's license and had registered the Caprice in New Jersey—both well outside the hot zone. And the FBI simply didn't have the type of software that could determine which vehicles' tags had been checked repeatedly by police officers from different jurisdictions. A crash effort by FBI technicians to develop that software would finally pay off, but not until the very last days of the investigation, on October 22. The new software program would reveal that Muhammad's battered Caprice was one of sixty vehicles that had been stopped by different police departments repeatedly in the area. "This was the first time," Gary Bald said, "that this information was available."

Maryland State Police Lieutenant Reichenbaugh's team worked on a similar effort, tweaked just a bit. In the weeks to come, when the sniper continually escaped police dragnets, investigators also decided to see if any vehicles were repeatedly stopped by police within one hour of each shooting. Through their Case Explorer software, detectives found that universe was fairly small—just eight cars. The 1990 Chevrolet Caprice was not among them.

But later, in the final days of the case, increasingly frustrated detectives expanded the search to within two hours of each shooting. The Caprice was there.

9

Getting Through
Another Rush Hour

When Gary Bald asked to have the renowned Behavioral Sciences Unit at the FBI Academy in Quantico, Virginia, produce a psychological profile of the person or persons behind the sniper shootings, he couldn't have been happier than when he learned that the specialist assigned to the task—FBI veteran Steve Etter—was himself a former sniper. Much has been made of the business of profiling, much of it nonsense. Many practitioners concede it is often more art than science, but investigators working even routine crimes like to have as many tools in the bag as possible. The profile prepared for Bald was just five pages. "Profile is really a misnomer," Bald said. The term of art the Bureau favors is "assessment."

Whatever they called it, the five-page document was among the closely held secrets of the sniper investigation. Only Bald, Chief Moose and a handful of other top officials knew its detailed contents. The disclosure of the tarot card message had infuriated Moose, Bald, ATF's Bouchard, and their colleagues. The sniper had attempted to open a dialogue with them and had said not to release the card's existence to the media. The leak to the press could have been interpreted as a curt brush-off, an insult. If the sniper got wind of the fact that Moose and the other top officials in the investigation were walking around with some kind of strange psychological profile in their vest pockets, it might drive him around the bend or, worse, provoke an angry spasm of new killings.

The profiler from Quantico examined patterns from past sniper cases and visited every sniper shooting scene in the Washington, D.C., case. Within the Behavioral Sciences Unit, it was received wisdom—and well-documented wisdom at that—that most snipers, almost all of them, are loners. But the author of the five-page document commissioned by Bald was unwilling to rule out a historical anomaly. "If it was more than one [person]," Bald said, paraphrasing loosely from the still-secret document, "there is going to be a person who is clearly dominant and [one] who is clearly subservient." Something to think about.

Past sniper shootings have tended to be committed by white men, but on the subject of the race of the possible shooters in D.C., the FBI document was mum. The twenty-four-hour cable networks were featuring nonstop marathons of all manner of psychiatric specialists, forensics scholars, even several former profilers from the Behavioral Sciences Unit at Quantico. The conventional wisdom, inasmuch as there was any, was that the shooter had to be a lone white male, a loser, perhaps a former military man disillusioned with the way things were going in the country. "The race of the shooters, we never discussed it," Bald said flatly. "We never even discussed it internally."

It was not a matter of being politically correct, several people involved in the investigation said. It was simply that such discussions were not just unhelpful but potentially harmful. "We didn't want [such a discussion] to taint the investigators," Bald said. What they wanted—and Moose was highly insistent on this point, several key officials said—was for the investigators to follow the evidence wherever it led. Period.

That said, Bald and others thought enough of the analysis in the five-page paper from Quantico that he added Etter's phone numbers to his speed dial and found himself consulting with him often. With so few clues to work with, it was helpful to test ideas and theories.

Especially given the fact that Etter himself had been a sniper.

The profilers and FBI negotiators advised the people standing behind the podium on what to say and how to say it, in the belief that everything said from that platform was being watched on television by the sniper. (The unnerving thought also crossed people's minds that the sniper might even be standing in the media throng in the parking lot at Montgomery County's police headquarters.) The profilers and negotiators helped Chief Moose, Bald and Bouchard craft statements to the sniper as they hammered out their messages for an hour or so before press conferences, sitting at Moose's handsome octagonal table in his office.

For instance, the day after the shooting of thirteen-year-old Iran Brown, when the public still didn't know about the tarot card, Moose made a coded comment to the shooter that echoed the "I am God" phrase on the card. From the podium, the chief said: "You should understand that I hope to God that some-day we'll know why all of this occurred," words suggested by the FBI profilers. Montgomery County School Superintendent Jerry Weast's appearances at the podium were limited after the shooting at the school. Better to pull back on public remarks having to do with schools, the FBI profilers and negotiators advised. Instead, the superintendent's communications about school safety would be through letters sent home to parents.

Besides helping to craft messages, some law enforcement officials found the profiler's words useful in devising investigative steps. For instance, days after a shooting in Virginia, the profiler went to the scene with the police chief and told the chief that the shooter or shooters were "hiding in plain sight." The chief interpreted this to mean the sniper "might have been hanging around" under their very noses, and he seized on that to come up with investigative strategies.

Besides behavioral profilers, police drew on other experts. They brought in Kim Rossmo, the research director of the nonprofit, Washington-based Police Foundation. Rossmo is a former detective inspector from Vancouver, British Columbia, who has worked with the Royal Canadian Mounted Police in producing what he calls "geoprofiles" of criminals. These are computer-generated analyses of where a killer may live and where he may attack next. Geoprofiles have been used to help solve serial crimes in Canada, the United Kingdom and the United States—crimes ranging from murder and rape to bombings, arsons and credit-card fraud. Working with members of the sniper task force, Rossmo's researchers examined all of the shooting sites and reviewed investigators' findings. "Crimes occur fairly close to an offender's home," Rossmo explained. "But not too close." Many criminals operate in a comfort zone, but they also want anonymity, he said. Street investigators poohpoohed the geographic profile, but the brass viewed it as one more tool, suggesting possible neighborhoods where the sniper lived. "It's a maybe," says Bouchard. "None of us relied on that and got tunnel vision."

While those profiles were viewed as valuable tools, all the leaders of the investigation were angry with the chorus of TV profiler pundits. At one of his press conferences two days after Iran Brown had been shot, Moose had harsh words for former cops turned commentators. He didn't name names but was speaking broadly. "Unfortunately, we have any number of talking heads in the media, retired police professionals, and you know, as a police professional, it is very insulting when there are retired police professionals because we know that they've not been briefed. They have not seen any of the evidence. They've not talked to any investigators. . . . They're ranting and raving on all of the various stations. They're telling people in the community information about the age, and therefore those people are, again, starting to have a closed mind about calling us and giving us information because they've heard someone on TV say that this is the age. . . . If they're putting people in this community at risk so that they can have the pleasure of being on TV, it is so sad because at one point they did really have a commitment to law enforcement," the chief said. "But what I'm seeing is an absolute ego problem. They are no longer anybody, but they do have the media in America, and that all of a sudden makes them somebody again. And it really is sad. So I feel sorry for them. But I also plead with them to stop. . . . We've got retired police chiefs out there looking for other jobs, taking advantage of this situation to get their face on television. How sad. How insulting."

Gary Bald actually got word to some of the TV talking heads to back off. "It was a concern because it was wrong," he said. "The parameters were undercut by the talking heads. And this was from people who knew better." Bald didn't read an article or watch TV during the investigation but relied on his media representative, Barry Maddox, to keep him posted. Some pundits apologized after they had been spoken to, and Maddox told Bald things had improved. Mike Bouchard, however, estimates the leaders of the investigation spent a quarter of their time trying to correct misinformation and telling people to keep an open mind. "All the private profilers on TV were misleading the public," he said. "They were telling people this is the kind of guy the cops are looking for. Then, we would have to go out and do damage control."

On Wednesday, October 9, Dean Harold Meyers was approaching a Sunoco station on Sudley Road just south of the hallowed Civil War battlefield at Manassas, Virginia, when he decided to fill the tank of his gray Mazda. It was a miserable night, and Meyers, a lifelong bachelor, fifty-three years old, had a long commute home to Maryland.

A soft-spoken civil engineer, a Vietnam veteran and inveterate Philadelphia Phillies fan, Meyers was standing in the narrow space between the gas pumps and his car when an unseen bullet struck him in the head at 8:18 P.M.

He died on the spot.

Meyers was the ninth person shot by the sniper, the seventh fatally. This was the eighth shooting in a busy retail area, the third at a gas station, the third close to a highway interchange.

A different pattern seemed to be emerging. But what kind?

Police immediately put out an all-points bulletin for a white Dodge Caravan with two men inside. A witness had seen such a vehicle leaving the area. The next morning, the description was refined to a white minivan, a panel vehicle, meaning it had only front windows.

Later that day, however, police ruled out that van as suspicious. Prince William County Police Chief Charlie Deane, whose jurisdiction includes Manassas, complained of "confusion about white vans." After that van was cleared, one federal law enforcement official said, he knew then that there was no white van involved in the shootings—but he was in a minority, he said, and his views were drowned out by hysteria about white vans. "These guys [the snipers] are very fortunate there are so many white vans out there," he said.

Since the shooting in Virginia's Spotsylvania County and the attack on Iran Brown in Prince George's County, Maryland, there wasn't a cop in the metropolitan Washington area for whom the sniper wasn't top of mind. In his Prince William jurisdiction,

Chief Deane had done some advance planning for the possibility the sniper might come his way. Earlier that Wednesday, the fifty-seven-year-old Deane had participated in two telephone conference calls with other area chiefs and briefed his staff about contingency plans.

After he got the call about the shooting at the Sunoco station, Deane raced from his home to the scene, ordering a swift and immense response. His officers moved quickly. So did other departments. In all, within minutes, between two hundred and three hundred local police and federal agents were blanketing the highways around the Sunoco station. Members of the sniper task force scene rushed in, even though supervisors literally had forced some agents and officers to go home and rest. "They're so determined to solve this case, that they volunteered, they've worked double shifts, they've done whatever has been asked of them," ATF Special Agent Harold Scott told reporters.

In Manassas, cops shut down the busy intersection around the gas station. Virginia State Police immediately shut down ramps to Interstate 66, one of the most heavily traveled commuter highways between suburban Virginia and Washington. Troopers began pulling over white vans up and down the highway. Detectives and troopers fanned out to find witnesses. Investigators thought the sniper might have hidden in the darkness in a wooded area about fifty to seventy-five yards behind the gas station. Believing that he had fired from a great distance, they searched a vast area for evidence, using flashlights that night and searching again the next morning. They also pulled surveillance tapes from nearby restaurants and gas stations, hoping they might yield a fleeting image of a person, his car, anything at all to go on. Police also got the airspace over the crime scene restricted to lessen noise from news media helicopters.

But there was nothing—nothing but a monstrous traffic jam in the Commonwealth of Virginia that would take hours to sort out.

And, once again, investigators were left with the sorry task of examining the life of the victim, even though it had become clear that this was so much not about the victims but about their killer.

For the family of the deceased, the pain and shock were unbearable.

Dean Meyers had grown up with three brothers in a white stucco Cape Cod in farm country outside Philadelphia. The Meyers boys spent hours on the baseball diamond they made in the backyard. He was a little shy in high school, loved tinkering with cars then and never struggled to get good grades. About to be drafted, he enlisted in the army instead. He never talked much about his time in Vietnam, but his brothers knew he had done reconnaissance missions. He only talked about the war once with his brother Greg. "It was a kind of rude awakening," Dean Meyers told him. On his first mission, his platoon was crossing a field surrounded by woods, and a sniper started shooting at them. The soldiers fell into the high grass, trying to figure out where the shots were coming from. Another time, he was nearly killed in an ambush, shot in the left arm above his elbow. He came home with a badly injured arm. He had an operation that moved the tendons in his wrist to the top of his hand, and after months of physical therapy, he was able to play sports again.

After the war, Meyers returned to the family and attended Penn State. He moved away after accepting a job in Washington, but he remained close to his brothers and talked to his elderly parents for an hour or so every weekend. On visits, he took his parents out to eat and helped with chores around the house. A project manager in the Manassas office of Dewberry and Davis, a civil engineering firm, Meyers had a strong work ethic, arriving at work early and leaving late. He loved the job so much that when he talked about retirement with his brothers, he'd say, "They'd have to kick me out."

Outside the office, Meyers had many interests: canoeing, water skiing, softball, tennis, and driving a motorcycle. He liked visiting historical sites and had a set of books about the Civil War. He loved old, hot cars—he once owned a 1968 Z28 light metallic blue Camaro, a 1966 dark blue Corvette convertible, a 1932 Ford three-window coupe with a 327 engine. The old Ford was painted orange and misted in black, and he got it from a guy nicknamed "Puff." The car was called "Puff's Wild Carrot." And just over the gas tank, it read "Carrot juice only."

Meyers lived alone in a townhouse in Gaithersburg, Maryland, for twenty-five years. He had no children, but was "Uncle Dean," the generous uncle to nine nephews and two nieces. He loved taking them on overnight camping and canoeing trips and giving them rides in his vintage Corvette, which he stored near the family home. He had a soft spot for kids. When he was in Vietnam, he used to pass out candy to children whenever his platoon came through rural hamlets. After his death, his family learned that he had sponsored children through World Vision, an international Christian humanitarian group. "I considered him a great brother and a best friend," said Greg Meyers. "I always felt comfortable confiding in him. If he didn't have the answer, he would tell you."

Thursday, October 10, marked the first full week since the sniper's spate of shootings on October 3. To many in the Washington area, it seemed a hellish eternity.

The FBI tip line had received about eight thousand calls, but Chief Moose told reporters they were still trying to prioritize the flow of information. Ordinary citizens, he added, should still be encouraged to call in any information they thought might be helpful.

At a briefing, a reporter asked Moose whether there would be extra security at Sunday's Washington Redskins game. The chief was thinking about just making it through each day—Sunday seemed a long way away. "I want to be forward thinking," the chief replied. "We also tend to think: Can we make it through the start of school, through the rush hour?"

Above: With each sniper shooting, pumping gas became an increasingly frightening activity. People came up with their own ways to try to put gas in their tanks safely. Here, a man in Rockville, Maryland, ducks behind his car.
(Olivier Douliery—ReflexNews)

Opposite, top: FBI agents and local officers search for clues near an Exxon gas station in Spotsylvania County, Virginia. Kenneth Bridges, a father of six, was killed while refueling his car on his way home to Philadelphia. (Jim Lo Scalzo—*U.S. News & World Report*)

Opposite, bottom: A Montgomery County police officer inspects a vehicle at a roadblock on Connecticut Avenue, a block from the early-morning shooting that killed bus driver Conrad Johnson on October 22 as he stood in his bus on Grand Pre Road in the Aspen Hill area near Silver Spring, Maryland.
(Cliff Owen—*The Washington Times*)

Opposite, top: Police stand near the body of Linda Franklin, who was shot at the Home Depot in Seven Corners Shopping Center in Falls Church, Virginia, on Monday, October 14, 2002. (Gerald Herbert—*The Washington Times*)

Opposite, bottom: Prince George's police officers guard buses at Benjamin Tasker Middle School on October 9, 2002, in Bowie, Maryland, two days after a sniper wounded thirteen-year-old Iran Brown there. (Stephen Jaffe—AFP)

Above: At a press conference after the arrests, Montgomery County Police Chief Charles Moose said investigators' work was continuing. (Nicholas Roberts)

Victims. Top row, left to right: Kenneth Bridges, James "Sonny" Buchanan, Pascal Charlot; middle row: Linda Franklin, Lori Lewis-Rivera, James Martin; bottom row: Dean Meyers, Premkumar Walekar, Conrad Johnson.

A restaurant window in Silver Spring, Maryland, was shattered by the bullet that killed thirty-four-year-old Sarah Ramos on October 3, 2002. She was an immigrant from El Salvador and the mother of a seven-year-old boy. (Manuel Ceneta—Gamma)

Lee Boyd Malvo, seventeen, left, and John Allen Muhammad, forty-one, are seen in happier times in this family photo taken in 2002 in Louisiana. The photo was provided by Muhammad's former sister-in-law Sheron Norman after the pair's arrest on Thursday, October 24, 2002, in Baton Rouge. (Polaris)

10

The Terror Is Here

At 9:30 A.M., Friday, October 11, the sniper struck again.

The morning rush hour had just about petered out. It was a misty, gray morning, and Spotsylvania County Sheriff Ronald L. Knight was out patrolling. His deputies were setting up a command trailer at the Spotsylvania Mall, where the woman had been wounded in front of the Michaels craft store exactly a week before. The deputies were going to question people at the mall to see if they remembered seeing anything strange the week before. Knight was driving his cruiser on Route 3, checking on schools, deviating from his normal route, which would have taken him directly past the Exxon station that morning. Then he got a call: A person shot at the Exxon station. Here we go again, Knight thought.

The sniper had been stalking yet another gas station, this time the Exxon on Route 1 in Four-Mile

Fork, Virginia, fifty miles south of Washington. The sniper was thumbing his nose at the cops: A uniformed Virginia state trooper was working a minor fender bender only fifty yards from the gas station. The sniper had fired anyway. The trooper heard the shot and ran to help the fallen man. He got there in less than a minute, but it was too late. He saw no one. The sniper was gone. Again. "Obviously, we're dealing with an individual that is extremely violent and obviously doesn't care," Spotsylvania County Sheriff's Maj. Howard Smith said.

Kenneth Bridges had stopped to fill his rented silver Buick before he drove home to Philadelphia. He was on his way home from a business meeting to take his daughter to the dentist. He called his wife, Jocelyn, from the service station to say he was on his way home. Other times that week, she had pleaded with him to please be careful. Five minutes after they spoke, Bridges was shot in the back. The fifty-three-year-old businessman was pronounced dead at Mary Washington Hospital.

All day, the TV cable news shows replayed the haunting image of the gas pump nozzle hanging from his tank, a grim reminder that stopping for gas was no longer a safe or perhaps even sensible activity.

Bridges, however, wasn't one to let fear rule his life. In so many ways, the lives of Kenneth Bridges and John Muhammad couldn't have been more different. Bridges was a father of six. His children ranged in age from twelve to twenty-four. "He was the kind of father interested in investing in his children," said friend Gary Shepherd. He and his family lived in a large stone house on a tree-lined street in the Philadelphia neighborhood of East Germantown. The couple was always together, riding their bikes, bagging leaves, having fun. He called Jocelyn "My Queen" and told people, "She keeps me straight."

Charismatic and energetic, Bridges for years had given motivational speeches and advocated African-American economic empowerment by encouraging black people to buy products from black-owned businesses. Black self-sufficiency, he believed, could be achieved by encouraging African Americans to spend their money in their own community. In 1997, he had cofounded MATAH Network, a distribution firm based in Oaklyn, New Jersey, near Camden, aimed at improving African-American businesses. "He dedicated his life to changing the conditions psychologically and economically of black folks," said friend Gaston Armour, MATAH's representative in Chicago. "He wanted to stop the drugs and crime in our neighborhoods. He would say that if you understood who you are as a black person, then you can help the black community and then help the community at large." As MATAH's executive vice president, Bridges believed that blacks still suffered from the psychological pain of slavery. With his resonant voice, Bridges preached his message to churches and community organizations around the country. He traveled almost every week, constantly working his cell phone. When he wasn't on the road, he would hug colleagues when he came into the company office. A favorite expression was, "My brother, show me some love. How you be?" Another favorite saying was "Let's get busy."

That was a motto he had applied to his own life. After graduating from Hillsdale College in 1971, Bridges earned an M.B.A. from the Wharton School of Business at the University of Pennsylvania. He worked in the marketing department at Scott Paper and became an Amway distributor on the side. He built a large, thriving Amway distributorship with more than three thousand distributors across the country. He left a comfortable salary at Scott in 1980 to pursue his Amway enterprise full-time. Bridges's friends speculated that he probably felt constrained in corporate America. He told friends he left Amway in frustration in 1983 when he couldn't persuade executives to sell more products from black-owned companies. In 1984, Bridges and a friend, Al Wellington, formed a business called P.O.W.E.R.—People Organizing and Working for Economic Rebirth—a direct-sales outfit aimed at distributing goods made by African Americans. The Reverend Louis Farrakhan was its national spokesman. A year later, they realized the time wasn't right for such a business, and Bridges went on to other things. But Bridges and Wellington teamed up after the Million Man March in October 1995—an event that John Muhammad told friends he had attended—and created a black distribution network that later evolved into MATAH.

Bridges's personal relationships with other people could not have been more different from those of Muhammad. In 1993, Bridges wrote a small book called *Succeeding in the World, Without Being of the World.* And in its dedication to his wife, he wrote, "Any doubts that God loved me were forever removed when he allowed me to have you as my wife. What a blessing!" To his parents, he wrote, "You gave me direction, encouraged me to have goals and made sure that I always had a plan. The best way for me to show you my thanks is to duplicate you with my children."

He had been in central Virginia for a meeting that resulted in clinching a big deal for MATAH with Dudley Products, the black-owned manufacturers of Grenada Nutmeg Oil, a natural topical pain reliever. He was elated, and the night before his death, he spoke with some of his MATAH colleagues by phone for more than two hours, telling them it was a "gee whiz" product that was going to put MATAH on the map.

Bridges was the tenth person to be struck by the sniper, the eighth fatality. It was the ninth shooting in a congested commercial area, the fourth at a gas station, and the fourth close to a major highway interchange.

The numbers, the pattern of shootings—if there was a method to the madness it was unclear to the army of police chasing the faceless sniper.

And the sniper, it seemed, was nowhere to be found.

Witnesses said they saw a white Chevrolet Astro van with a ladder rack on top leaving the scene. They said two people were in the van, that it was heading toward Route 1 and Interstate 95, possible escape routes. The police put out a BOLO—a be-on-the-lookout alert—for the white van, though the Spotsylvania County sheriff's office stressed that it had not been directly linked to the shooting. Also, no one had a tag number.

In flak jackets, sheriff's deputies and Virginia State Police mounted a massive dragnet. They shut down Route 1 and blocked ramps to Interstate 95. Guns drawn, officers stopped and searched hundreds of white vans on the highways, some as far away as

Baltimore County, Maryland. It created gridlock for hours, especially along Interstate 95, as drivers waited to clear police checkpoints. In some spots, they funneled the traffic down to one lane. The spectacle was carried live on national television. But as the minutes ticked by, hopes fell, and it was apparent that the sniper had slipped away. Again. And the region braced for yet more random shootings. Col. W. Gerald Massengill, the Virginia State Police superintendent, told reporters that the roadblocks had been erected "obviously, not quick enough." He urged people not to focus only on white vans. "We don't want preconceived notions out there," he said. "But certainly . . . you have to play the hand that you're dealt. And the information that has come to us deals with white vans. So we're still interested in white vans."

Just the sight of a white van was enough to panic some people. Once, they were just part of the passing landscape, hardly noticed by anyone. Now, they stood out like an evil wheeled totem. But privately some investigators were saying people perhaps were being conditioned to see a white van after the shootings because of all the attention they had gotten.

In the stop-and-start rain, nine ATF agents methodically worked a grid search through the parking lot of a Ramada Inn across the street from the Exxon station. Clad in navy blue windbreakers, the agents formed a dark line as they stood shoulder to shoulder and then took small steps across the blacktop searching for evidence. More ATF agents closely inspected bushes some fifty yards from the shooting, sawing off limbs and using metal detectors. Investigators searched through the grass, placing a yellow piece of paper in a bag at one point, though investigators later wouldn't say what the paper was. Detectives knocked on doors at about a half-dozen motels and questioned at least a hundred people to determine if they had seen anything suspicious. Investigators canvassed businesses. Officers also asked for tapes from a surveillance camera at a nearby Citgo station. By midafternoon, a helicopter had taken bullet fragments to the ATF's Rockville lab. The geoprofilers also swooped onto the scene to see how the latest shooting might fit into a computerized profile about where the shooter might live. As the sun set in an amber sky, Spotsylvania Sheriff Knight walked toward the gas station. "This sixty-year-old sheriff is damn tired," he said.

At 8:30 P.M., the ATF confirmed what everyone already knew: the ballistics evidence matched the other shootings in Virginia, Maryland and Washington. This latest shooting ratcheted up the fear in the region still higher. Authorities urged people to go on with their lives, but many were simply too afraid. The police urged calm. They asked residents to keep calling with tips. The call was answered in spades. From noon until midnight that Friday, the Spotsylvania sheriff's office received more than one thousand nine hundred telephone calls. Forty calls a minute poured into the police department's communications center. Calls to the FBI tip line came at an even more furious pace—about a thousand calls an hour. As they came in, investigators tried to prioritize them, logging them in, reviewing the leads, trying to sort out which ones should be deemed top priorities and which could wait. But it was almost impossible to discern the few legitimate calls from the mountain of frantic sightings of white vans and suspicions about gun-happy neighbors.

Anytime there are few explanations for virtually any frightening or mystifying national tragedy in American history, conspiracy theories offer people something to grab onto. In the absence of facts, even fleeting theories are comforting. They are a way for people to try to make sense of the incomprehensible. And the sniper siege, certainly, was no different. The country was still recovering from the 9/11 terrorist attacks from a year earlier, and the nation's capital, in particular, still had its guard up after the attack on the Pentagon and the anthrax-laced letters. Washington was still a city somewhat on edge, where almost anything suspicious was seen as a possible terrorist plot. During the sniper shootings, conspiracy theories flourished. For instance, some Washington residents suggested that perhaps the sniper attacks were a distracting prelude to another mass attack. Fairly early on, though, law enforcement dismissed the notion that this was the work of Osama bin Laden's minions. This wasn't the way al Qaeda did business. They wanted a big body count. Still, on Saturday, October 12, Spotsylvania Sheriff Ronald Knight was asked if the shootings were the calculated work of terrorists, and his answer addressed the anxiety. "The terror is here, and that is terrorism," he told reporters. "So whether it's a local terrorist or a global terrorist, I don't want to say. But you know it is striking terror in people's hearts."

The sniper hadn't struck the weekend before, and all week, the TV pundits had been remarking that the

Above: Going out to dinner no longer seemed safe. Here, federal and local law enforcement agents stand outside the Ponderosa steak house in Ashland, Virginia, where a man was shot and wounded Saturday night, October 19, 2002. (James Estrin—*The New York Times*)

Opposite: Bus driver Conrad Johnson, a father of two, had a loyal following of riders. Here, passengers look at a makeshift memorial at the bus stop where Johnson was shot and killed October 22, 2002. (Mark Wilson—Getty Images)

Opposite: Investigators comb the yard of a Tacoma, Washington, home Wednesday, October 23, 2002, looking for evidence. (Lui Kit Wong—*The News Tribune*/Corbis Sygma)

Left: Police sketch of a suspect in the shooting of two liquor store employees on September 21, 2002, in Montgomery, Alabama. (Montgomery Police Department)

Below: Law enforcement officers surround the car that John Muhammad and Lee Boyd Malvo were in when police arrested them at a rest stop on October 24, 2002. (Brendan McDermid—Reuters)

Above: Montgomery, Alabama, Police Chief John Wilson answers questions about the shooting that occurred outside the liquor store behind him on September 21, 2002. Police said Lee Malvo's fingerprint was found on a gun catalog dropped during a chase. (Dave Martin—AP)

Right, top: Claudine Parker, fifty-two, was shot and killed as she locked up the liquor store that night.

Right, bottom: Co-worker Kellie Adams, twenty-four, also was shot below her skull that night. The bullet came out through her chin. (Dave Martin—AP)

Above: A Tucson, Arizona, police officer stands by his car in a practice area of the Fred Enke Golf Course, looking at the area where the body of Jerry R. Taylor, sixty, was found March 19, 2002.
(Benjie Sanders—*The Arizona Daily Star*)

Left, top: Keenya Cook, twenty-one, was shot and killed with a handgun on February 16, 2002, when she opened the door of her aunt's home in Tacoma, Washington. Her aunt, Isa Nichols, had sided against John Muhammad in a custody dispute.

Left, bottom: Jerry R. Taylor loved golf.

Above: Carol Williams and her friend Vince Hutchinson leave the news conference in front of her home in Baton Rouge, Louisiana, on October 24, 2002. She is John Allen Muhammad's first ex-wife. (Bill Feig—AP)

Right: Mildred Muhammad, John Muhammad's second ex-wife, moved to Clinton, Maryland, with their three children. Some investigators believe that's why he came to the D.C. suburbs. (Dudley M. Brooks—*The Washington Post*)

Above: John Allen Muhammad poses with a rifle during his days in the Louisiana National Guard. (Polaris)

Left: A 1997 picture of Lee Boyd Malvo from Spalding High School in Jamaica. (Spalding High School—ZUMA)

Above, left: John Allen Muhammad arrives in the Prince William Circuit Court. (Dave Ellis—AP/Pool) **Above, right: Lee Boyd Malvo is escorted from juvenile court in Fairfax, Virginia.** (Lawrence Jackson—AP)

Below: At Children's Hospital, First Lady Laura Bush sits with thirteen-year-old Iran Brown. (Alex Wong—Getty Images)

sniper seemed to take weekends off. Toward the work-week's end, many people were wary about the week-end. But then, after Friday's shooting at the Exxon station, cancellations poured in from everywhere. One by one, outdoor weekend sporting events and Friday night football games—even homecoming games—were nixed. Schools were locked down again. Some people were resorting to walking down side-walks in a zigzag line—the theory, at least, being that you somehow were less of a target if you were weaving. People adopted new methods of pumping gas—either sitting in the car, hiding behind the pumps, or topping off so they didn't have to stop as often. One woman offered to buy a coworker lunch if he would pump gas for her. Some out-of-towners temporarily staying in the Washington region for work would use the prepaid gas option with rental cars to avoid the pumps.

Gas stations weren't the only places suddenly off-limits. Normally bucolic spots such as pumpkin patches were taboo. Jean Phillips owned a favorite fifteen-acre pumpkin patch in northern Montgomery County. On the morning of October 3, she took a group of three- and four-year-olds for a hayride. After-ward, the children, their teachers and all their just-picked pumpkins were spread out on the ground at the edge of the woods. They were picnicking when a call came to tell them about the sniper. They were ordered back to school. That was the last group Phillips had during the sniper spree. No one wanted to take a chance. "We had one hundred percent can-cellations," said Phillips. Normally, she would get about two thousand kids every October; in 2002, she had just thirty. No birthday parties, scout meetings or church outings at the pumpkin patch. Grocers cut back their orders, too. "They said customers didn't want to carry anything that would slow them down," she said. Phillips tried to salvage the season by bringing pumpkins to school, but that took twice as long and brought in less than half as much.

The sense of dread was palpable. One mother summed up the feelings. "I can usually separate myself from the bad things that are happening to other people, as if I am watching a bad movie. Not this time," said Mara Bayewitz, a mother of two who lived four miles from Aspen Hill, where several of the shootings occurred in Montgomery County. "This sniper makes me feel like a walking, breathing target all the time." She routinely grabbed a paper bag to steady her breathing and peered into wooded areas as she drove, looking all around her. "Everyone I know feels this way," she said. "We all dive into our cars from the grocery store parking lot. We all feed our kids sandwiches or cereal instead of running out to the store to get food for dinner. We all feel a sense of relief when the sniper strikes because on some level we know where he is and we can feel safe for at least an hour or two. And we all feel guilty for feeling that way."

President Bush was following the sniper case closely, receiving daily updates. "The president's going to continue to monitor this very closely and make certain that the government is doing everything it can and should to help," White House Press Secretary Ari Fleischer told reporters. Through the weeks of the crisis, Bush was aware of the criticism that he was not appearing to be actively involved in the investigation. But the FBI had told the White House that the president should not take a more visible role because that might lead the sniper to think he could communicate directly with the president of the United States. That, Bush was advised, might "empower the killer," which was the last thing the president wanted.

The strain of the ordeal was showing on investigators. During a press conference that Friday, October 11, Chief Moose said he and his men were continuing to work around the clock, putting all possible resources into it. "When I left home this morning— and I don't want to appear to be out of touch—but I do recall asking my wife what day it was, because it really doesn't matter," the chief said. "We're working every day, working hard." The ATF's Mike Bouchard said of those eighteen- and twenty-hour days, "Our minds were running one hundred miles an hour." He was working so hard and was so isolated working on the case, he said, that he almost didn't pick up on the fear in the community, a sentiment expressed by other law enforcement officers absorbed by the details of the investigation. One weekend, Bouchard had hockey tickets. He knew he needed to take a break and get some balance back in his life. He stepped away for a few hours to take his son to the game. A high school junior and avid sports fan, the younger Bouchard was worried about his dad's safety. Bouchard sought the right words to explain to his son and his college-age daughter what was happening. "There are crazy people out there, people who do strange things," the agent told them. "But there's more good than bad in the world. And the good guys will win in the end."

Despite himself, Bouchard couldn't help wondering when that might be.

The FBI's Gary Bald found himself so consumed by his responsibilities that he wasn't talking to people outside the investigation and was utterly removed from the level of fear paralyzing the region. He felt such an obligation to find the sniper that sometimes he found himself scanning the horizon when he was pumping gas. But not out of fear, he said: "I was trying to find the guy."

11

The Hottest Crime Story
Since O.J.

On Saturday, October 12, nine days after the sniper began his shooting spree during the morning rush hour in Montgomery County, Chief Moose released two composites to reporters. Ordinarily, when police resort to this measure during the course of an investigation, they release photographs of suspects. The composites Moose released were not of people but of a truck.

A white box truck, to be precise.

For all their efforts, for all the thousands of tips received, the tens of thousands of man-hours logged in the investigation since the shootings started, the army of law enforcement agents pursuing the snipers still had no idea who the gunman—or gunmen—was. They had no reliable eyewitness accounts of the shooter, a paltry but potentially valuable cache of ballistics evidence, and absolutely no idea why the sniper was killing people and when he might strike again.

What they did have were several witnesses who thought they had seen a white delivery truck near several of the first shootings in Montgomery County at the approximate times the shootings occurred. This was news, and the reporters seized on it like red meat. To date, the police had disclosed only that a white van or box truck had been seen in the vicinity of the bench where Sarah Ramos was shot near the Leisure World retirement community in Silver Spring, on October 3. Now Moose was saying that a similar vehicle had been spotted near more than one shooting that morning. And the composites had been assembled from the descriptions of several witnesses who claimed to have seen the vehicle.

It wasn't much as breakthroughs go. But it was something.

Playing the meager hand he had been dealt, Moose took pains to point out the details of the vehicle: a roll-up door in the rear, a dent in the rear bumper, oxidized paint, no gleam or sheen, large lettering on the side. No one had been able to give a license plate number. "Oftentimes, people may be confused by what they've seen, what they've heard, and we want to be very careful before we put a composite of this type out," the chief said. "We want to stress that we have witnesses from more than one location reporting this composite."

A reporter asked Moose if it was an error to concentrate on the color white for the vehicle, if this was impeding the investigation. "Well, sir, we're all welcome to our own opinion," Moose said. "Any other questions?"

The chief repeated that police were interested in the white Astro van seen leaving the shooting at the Exxon station in Spotsylvania County the day before, noting that they planned to do a composite on that vehicle too. "We're operating with a sense of urgency," he said, "but when you're dealing with witnesses, reinterviewing, letting their emotions—giving them downtime—all of those things that are necessary for people that are involved in this very traumatic series of incidents, sometimes it just takes time."

With the release of the photos on a Saturday, for the Sunday newspapers, the white box truck and the white van became even more embedded in people's minds. And at the same time, the chief hit on what might have been fueling the growing legend of the mysterious white box truck—the witnesses were people who had seen people shot and murdered in cold blood. Those were highly traumatic events that could easily distort memory.

Later in the day, Charles Ramsey, the police chief of neighboring Washington, D.C., disclosed to reporters that his detectives and patrol officers were looking for a burgundy, older model, four-door Chevrolet Caprice with tinted windows. The vehicle had been seen leaving the intersection where Pascal Charlot had been murdered on the night of October 3. The neighborhood in question was far from one of Washington's toniest, and there were plenty of junkers that traveled through that busy corner on the way to the Capital Beltway a couple of miles away. But the Caprice was of interest to police, Ramsey said, both because of the timing of its departure from the scene of the crime and because it had its lights off at the time. In all the focus on the white box truck and the Astro van, however, Ramsey's mention of the Caprice was buried in the next day's news reports.

Moose, for his part, was not wedded to the theory of the white box truck. Consulting, as he did every day, with the ATF's Mike Bouchard and the FBI's Gary Bald, he believed that investigators had to focus on the strongest leads they had. At the moment, that happened to be the eyewitness accounts of the white box truck and the ballistics evidence linking the shooters to a rifle that fired .223-caliber ammunition. If the investigators unearthed more compelling evidence that took the inquiry in another direction, the chief would be talking about that. For now, however, the emphasis was on the white box truck, and Moose saw no harm in saying so. "I do not feel that us following up an investigation and getting more information out about the white box truck that we're looking for limits anyone," Chief Moose said. Instead, he said, he had a different impression of what was happening in the community: "Everybody is looking at everything and everybody."

Asked if his department had reviewed previous shootings in Montgomery County to see if there were any similarities, the chief gave his standard answer. "Sir, we are continuing to conduct the investigation, and to talk about any of those specifics would be inappropriate."

Moose had been in the glare of the media spotlight almost nonstop for the past nine days, and he clearly was not enjoying the experience. But he still needed to be able to use the reporters and the TV cameras if he was going to be able to strike up any kind of meaningful dialogue with the sniper. That didn't mean that he was going to allow the media to screw up or impede his investigation, and at his Saturday news conference, the chief made the point in the most emphatic terms. What concerned Moose, Bald and Bouchard was that some reporters had begun following investigators as they paid calls on people who had called in anonymous tips—people who, for obvious reasons, very much wanted to remain anonymous. "We ask you to please consider the fact that you may jeopardize this very critical investigation," Moose told the assembled throng of reporters and TV news crews. "You may jeopardize the safety of our investigators. You may actually be compromising our witnesses."

The reporters listened silently. Those who had covered a police beat knew the validity of what Moose had said. But the sniper story had become too big, the media circus unmanageable. It wasn't just the local press that was in the hunt. The national press, the cable networks, foreign TV crews—this was the hottest crime story since O.J., and no local police, no matter how well meaning, were going to contain its coverage.

The tension between the media and law enforcement underscored the fact that neither had much to go on. They were all scrambling, cops and reporters alike. The police, of course, had the job of finding the sniper and putting him out of business; the reporters had a major story to cover.

The gulf, in the end, would be unbridgeable.

Moose, through it all, put on a brave public face. Were the task force investigators feeling frustrated? Not frustrated, he said, but feeling that there was work to do. "People who are working on the investigation are very compassionate," Moose said. "We have people being assaulted, being killed, and that doesn't please any of us. That tells us that we need to continue to work harder. That means we need to do everything in our power to make sure that nothing is compromised. That means to make sure that we need to focus, focus, focus." And that means, he said, that investigators couldn't even talk to their families about the case. The risks were too great. "If someone says something that then appears in public, that slows us down," he said, "and causes us all to alter some progress, then that is unfortunate."

Asked if he had a message for the gunman, Moose said, "The message remains the same: 'To think about what you're doing and turn yourself in to law enforcement.' "

The chief adjourned the news conference moments later.

Of course, no one knew if the sniper had been listening to Moose's words. But no one really believed he would heed them if he had heard them.

Day twelve, Sunday, October 13, was quiet.

The FBI tip line was swamped. Callers reported getting repeated busy signals. At a morning news conference, Chief Moose asked the reporters to remind the public that the tip line's area code was 888, not 800. The 800 number many callers had been dialing belonged to a private corporation. The calls were wreaking havoc on the business. Moose also noted that so many people had been trying to get the composite of the white box truck off the Internet that one of the Web sites had crashed. Technicians had fixed the problem, and the image was available on the FBI, ATF and Montgomery County Police Department Web pages.

There wasn't much else to announce, but the chief reiterated his plea to the public: Someone who had been in the area of a shooting might have seen the white truck. Someone might have seen someone repairing the damage to the truck's rear bumper. Someone might have noticed the truck being painted. "Maybe you weren't there that day," the chief said, "but [you may] have some knowledge, have some association with this vehicle."

Even on a slow day, there were leads that sent the blood racing. In Gaithersburg, not far from the site of Moose's press conference in Rockville, a man in a white Astro van was detained near a pool hall. Police discovered a rifle inside. A quick investigation showed the man could not have been the sniper. Asked about the incident, Moose said only, "There is a lot of police work that is ongoing."

That afternoon, Moose, Mike Bouchard, Gary Bald, and Montgomery County Executive Doug Duncan went on CNN's *Late Edition*. Veteran correspondent Wolf Blitzer asked the law enforcement trio about an older model, burgundy Chevrolet Caprice that had been seen leaving the area where Pascal Charlot had been killed on October 3. "I think there's been more law enforcement focus on that," Moose said noncommittally, [but] not a big push for public feedback about that." The white box truck, in other words, still trumped all other leads.

Duncan, the county's top elected official, had been the reassuring voice at the podium for the community. The cops talked about the investigation—or not. And Duncan was the point man for the community. Blitzer asked him what advice he had for residents as they went about their lives. "We're asking people, as best they can, go about your normal routine," Duncan said. "Make sure you go to work, make sure you send your kids to school." Those words might not sound terribly startling, but the fear was so strong, it was beginning to change the way people lived their lives.

Blitzer asked about a shooting that had occurred back in September at a liquor store in Silver Spring, Maryland, across the county from Moose's headquarters building in Rockville. Bouchard took the query. The ATF lab had examined the ballistics evidence from that shooting, he said. It had been deemed "inconclusive." Blitzer pressed the matter, asking if there were similarities between the Silver Spring shooting and the October sniper shootings. Bouchard, politely, declined to discuss the matter.

Next, it was Bald's turn in the spotlight. Was it possible, Blitzer asked, that the sniper shootings might be the work of al Qaeda terrorists? "We haven't ruled anything in," Bald said, his face unreadable as a blank chalkboard, "and we're not ruling anything out."

A quiet weekend was ending.

To millions of men, women and children preparing for another anxious week of work and school in the suburban Washington area, there was no ready evidence that police would catch the person or persons who had decided to impose this incomprehensible reign of terror on their communities. As the sheriff in Spotsylvania County, Virginia, had put it, if people are terrified, then whoever was responsible was a terrorist.

It was a handy enough definition.

But it sure didn't calm many nerves.

12

You'll Never Catch Me

Monday, October 14, was Columbus Day, a holiday for the many federal workers in the Washington, D.C., area, a long weekend filled with apprehensive anticipation.

Shortly before 2 P.M., standing on the South Lawn of the White House, President Bush spoke out strongly for the first time about the sniper, calling him "a sick mind who obviously loves terrorizing society." Bush would continue "lending all the resources of the federal government" to investigators, he said. "I'm just sickened, sick to my stomach, to think that there is a cold-blooded killer at home taking innocent life. The idea of moms taking their kids to school and sheltering them from a potential sniper attack is not the America I know."

Just over seven hours later, at about 9:15 P.M., the sniper struck again.

This time, it was outside a Home Depot store, just

forty-five minutes before closing time. The quiet weekend was, it was clear now, just a lull, a pause. The sniper would kill where and when he chose. And despite all their efforts, the police seemed utterly unable to stop him.

The Home Depot was located at the Seven Corners Shopping Center in Fairfax County, Virginia. The mall was located about six miles west of Washington, near what is arguably one of the busiest intersections on the entire East Coast. Boasting one of the nation's highest median household incomes, Fairfax County is a leafy suburb where thousands of comfortable, white-collar office workers live. Like Montgomery County across the Potomac River in Maryland, Fairfax residents experience very little in the way of criminals and criminal activity. In 2002, there were only sixteen homicides. In a county with just over a million people spread out over nearly four hundred square miles, it was among the lowest homicide rates in the nation.

The Home Depot shooting was yet another departure for the sniper.

Since his killing spree had begun on October 2, the sniper had chosen his kill zones carefully. Some of the past ones had had woods close by, allowing him to pick off his victims from distances so great no one could see him. The Seven Corners Shopping Center didn't offer that kind of cover. It's a strip mall with the same familiar suburban signposts: Dollar City, Starbucks, Ross Dress for Less. The mall didn't offer cover or a quick exit. The area around there was an obstacle course of stoplights and parking lots and state roads. The place was called Seven Corners for a reason. Among the roads that intersect there are several heavily traveled highways, like Virginia Routes 50 and 7. It's also a jump from Interstates 66 and 495, which could be getaway routes.

Like a lot of malls, designed to keep shoppers in front of the merchandise as long as possible, this one requires real thought to get in and out of. In addition, Home Depot's two-story, open-air parking garage has lots of concrete pillars and beams, lots of cars and a Chinese restaurant on one side. A very tricky target, in other words. It was almost as if the sniper were communicating with his pursuers through his choice of location for his attacks. Chief Moose, seeking to calm his community, had pointed out early on that schoolchildren seemed safe. Then, after the first quiet weekend since the killing spree began, young Iran Brown was gunned down right outside his school. In the week since, the murders of Dean Meyers and Kenneth Bridges had the media's and every water-cooler conversation dominated by the risk of pumping gas, particularly at stations by busy highways. Now the sniper had changed tack and tactics again.

You'll never catch me, he seemed to sneer.

Linda Franklin was standing near her husband, Ted, as he loaded shelving into their shiny red convertible on the ground floor of the confined parking garage when the sniper's bullet felled her. She was forty-seven, employed as a terrorism analyst for the FBI. It would seem the cruelest of ironies.

Born in Indiana, she moved with her family to Gainesville, Florida, when she was in middle school. Her father, Charles Moore, liked to joke that there was a time during her early years when he gladly would have given her up for adoption. "She was always pulling stunts that sometimes infuriated me," he said. Like the time she convinced her older sister that she was adopted. But everyone knew Linda wasn't malicious, just playful. After finishing high school in three years, Franklin took nurse's training but was so appalled at the treatment of the elderly in nursing homes that she quit. "That's when I found out I had a daughter with character," her father said. She went to work for a dentist, got married, moved a lot and had two children, Katrina and Thomas Belvin. The marriage broke up, and Linda, a single mother, moved back to Gainesville to attend college.

"I'll help you any way I can," her dad offered.

"You are not going to pay for my going through school," she replied.

There were times her father did lend her cash for books or tuition, but Franklin was diligent about keeping track of her debts. She repaid every dime.

She raised her two children alone, worked, went to the University of Florida in Gainesville and graduated with honors from its education school, where she focused on math and science. Franklin didn't speak any foreign languages, but she talked to one of her professors about working outside the country. Her first assignment was teaching the children of diplomats in Guatemala. The country was in such upheaval that Franklin and her two young children had an armed escort when they went out. One day, she was accosted by a machete-wielding man who demanded she give him the Jeep she was driving. Forget it, Franklin said. She was keeping the Jeep, but she would drive the man where he needed to go.

After that incident, Linda Franklin decided to return to Florida. An old professor suggested a job with the Department of Defense and gave her a letter of introduction. Her first job was in Germany, then Okinawa, where she taught high school for six years. Franklin, her father said, was a terrible tennis player, but the high school needed a tennis coach.

"You've got to be kidding," her astonished father told her.

"I don't have to play, I just need to teach," she replied.

She got herself a bunch of books about tennis. Her team ended up winning the league championship.

Okinawa is where she met Ted Franklin. They married in Hawaii. Soon afterward, they moved to Brussels, where Linda worked as a high school teacher at NATO. She and Ted got involved in an orphanage there, sharing Christmas with a red-haired child. The orphanage went to the military for Christmas support, and Linda was among the first to ask, "What else do you need?" She arranged for a memorable party—an American cookout, including a wooden gym set for the kids to play on.

The job Linda Franklin loved most was working for the FBI. She started there in 1998 and was an analyst in the National Infrastructure Protection Center, which investigates threats to utilities, banks, water supplies and public safety. Franklin was good at her job, her supervisors have said, but even more important, she had that rare and valued ability of making other employees feel comfortable.

Compassionate and humble, Franklin used to take care of the less fortunate. When she saw someone who looked hungry standing outside a store, she would buy something to eat and then have the owner give it to him. "She didn't want recognition for what she did," her father said. Her mother, Maryann Moore, said: "She fed and clothed the homeless. She was normal. She was not a saint, but she was close."

With a sparkling smile and blond hair, Linda Franklin was a tiny, outdoorsy girl who loved skiing, snow tubing, river-rafting, biking and hiking. She loved to fish but hated removing her catch from the hook. Every summer, she used to organize a big crowd of family and friends—sometimes as many as twenty people—for a camping trip near a big lake with cabins near Gainesville. "I don't remember a summer she didn't do it," said her father. "Everyone always wanted to be with Aunt Linda because she always had something up her sleeve." She loved watching adventure movies, like *Star Wars* flicks, with her husband and other couples. With two dogs and two cats, she was a softie for animals.

Franklin had known hardship before. Little more than a year before her death, she had had breast cancer and undergone a double mastectomy. "She wanted to be a survivor," her father said. "She didn't want to go through what her mother went through." She had seen how cancer had spread through her mother's body after she had been diagnosed with breast cancer. After her surgery, Franklin had breast reconstruction, but her recovery was difficult. Just walking up and down stairs was draining. She went to physical therapy four or five times a week, but she didn't let on how grueling it was. "She had the best attitude," said a good friend, Peggy Hulseberg. "She knew it was serious, but she was like, 'Hey, just get it taken care of.' She wouldn't impose on anyone to help her."

She had endured another sorrow in August when her eighteen-year-old niece was killed after flipping her car on a rain-slick road. They had been especially close, and Franklin was devastated by her death.

But she had something to look forward to. Her twenty-three-year-old daughter, Katrina Hannum, was expecting her first child, a boy, in February, making Franklin a grandmother for the first time.

Linda Franklin excelled at planning. And she had a lot of plans. She figured she would be involved in the government's big new homeland security effort. She and Ted, a computer network engineer, wanted eventually to build a house. They sold their condo and were planning to live temporarily in an apartment, which they were fixing up the night they came to Home Depot. "She had a lot of dreams," said her father. Now Charles Moore is writing his daughter's life story to share with her grandson someday. "She lived more in those forty-seven years," her mother said, "than many people live in a lifetime."

"Someone was shot!" a man in the parking garage screamed.

"Someone got killed!" another yelled.

People ran into the Home Depot store. Many shouted to shut the door. Terrified customers in the front scrambled to the rear.

In the parking garage, Linda Franklin lay dead, her husband, Ted, by her side, their plans for the new home, for their future, shattered.

There are a few moments in history etched permanently in the memory of Tom Manger. The forty-seven-year-old chief of the Fairfax County Police Department, Manger recalls the day in second grade when he learned that President Kennedy had been shot. There was the moment he watched the second plane slam into the south tower of the World Trade Center on television, then looked outside to see smoke rising from the Pentagon.

The night Linda Franklin was murdered, Manger had just gotten home and was playing with his one-year-old son, a light moment after a long day at the office. Then, his pager beeped. The text message said: "Shooting at Home Depot. Seven Corners. Possible sniper-related."

Manger had had butterflies in his stomach day and night before then, worried—as were many police chiefs in the region—that their communities might be the sniper's next target. Glancing at his pager, Manger felt like someone had punched him in the gut. It was almost as if someone had just called to say one of his parents had died. His mind raced. "OK," he thought, "what do we have to do?" His department, like Chief Deane's to the southwest in Prince William County, Virginia, had done a lot of planning. It took Manger all of thirty seconds to climb back into his uniform. He raced over to Home Depot, siren blaring. When he got there, the place was crawling with cops. Before long, there would be more than two hundred of them there. Cops from all over just showed up. "Hey," one said, "we are here to help."

At a press conference very late that night, Manger told reporters: "I know the question on everyone's mind is: Is this shooting related to the others we've had in the area? It's too early to tell at this point.

However, we are working it and investigating it with that potential in mind."

Those were the words you had to say. In his heart, Manger knew exactly what he was dealing with. Now the sniper was his business, too.

Just as they did after Friday's shooting at the Exxon station, police quickly clamped down on roads and checked vehicles. The thinking was that this guy was probably fleeing up the Interstate toward Montgomery County. Rifle-toting officers shut down many roads and highways in Northern Virginia, and motorists cooled their heels in their cars for hours. The cops checked each car before permitting it to proceed in a single lane. They shut down most bridges leading from Virginia into Maryland and Washington, D.C. Officers closed part of the Capital Beltway. All the while, helicopters with high-powered beams whirred overhead. Meanwhile, legions of other officers cruised neighborhoods, looking for anything suspicious.

The first officers had appeared in minutes, but that wasn't fast enough. The sniper had slipped away again.

The dragnet was a huge inconvenience for motorists, but police said later that the public knew it was an imperfect plan. "Was it a long shot? Sure. Do we think it was worth doing? Absolutely," Manger said weeks later. "You needed to pull out all the stops."

Tensions were running high. Not long after the shooting, police got a taunting call warning of another shooting, in thirty minutes. The sniper hadn't issued warnings before, but then he had never shot anyone in a busy parking garage before, either. It was frightening.

Inside the garage, police officers crawled on their knees, searching for any bit of evidence. Crime-scene techs worked through the night, photographing, diagramming—trying to piece together the sniper's latest hellish chapter. The next day, police recruits walked shoulder to shoulder through the garage, scouring every square inch to make sure nothing had been overlooked.

Investigators also reviewed tapes from store surveillance cameras and traffic cameras on freeways—now a routine practice after every sniper shooting. Another standard step was pulling several days' worth of credit card purchases at gas stations around the site. This was another long shot, one that produced maybe a hundred thousand records. They were hoping for one credit card that might have shown up near several shooting sites. There was great excitement when they saw one card over and over near a number of locations. But it was only another dead end. It was a corporate credit card that employees of a private company had used to purchase gas. But it was a step that investigators couldn't afford to skip.

It may have been just a weird coincidence, but there was a Michaels craft store in the Seven Corners Shopping Center. At a time when there were no explanations for the madness, it was something some people latched on to. Two previous sniper shootings had occurred near Michaels stores.

There was something different about this shooting, however, besides the unlikely location. The sniper, so it seemed, had gotten careless. News reports said a witness had seen a gunman step from his van inside the parking garage, some ninety feet from Franklin and her husband. The *Washington Post* published a grim account of an individual who said another witness told him he had seen a man standing next to a light-colored van at the end of the aisle where Franklin's car was parked. He told police that he had seen the man hoist a gun to his shoulder and shoot Franklin. Then, he said, the man got into the van and drove off. Never before had the sniper been so close to his victims. The whole region hoped he was slipping up, emerging from the shadows.

Late that night, Chief Manger said several witnesses had provided license plate information. Witnesses said they saw a white or cream-colored Chevrolet Astro van with a silver ladder rack on top. It sounded an awful lot like the vehicle witnesses said they had seen leaving Friday morning's shooting of Ken Bridges at the Exxon station. Witnesses said the light-colored van seen at Home Depot had a malfunctioning rear taillight. "I am confident that ultimately that information is going to lead us to an arrest in this case," Manger told reporters.

It didn't get a lot of attention that night or in the following days, but some sketchy news reports that night said witnesses saw a dark, late-model Chevrolet or Chrysler suddenly back up and leave the scene. That sighting was lost in all the noise about white vans and box trucks.

Earlier Monday, before Linda Franklin was shot, a reporter asked Chief Moose whether the maroon Chevy Caprice seen speeding away from the District of Columbia shooting had been connected to the sniper case. "Sir, it would be inappropriate for me to talk about that part of the investigation," he said. No one was really looking for a Caprice. The FBI's Gary Bald explained weeks later that the description of the Caprice from the October 3 shooting of Pascal Charlot was vague. Bald also said that police tried to be careful to say that witnesses had described seeing the white box trucks and white vans in the area of the shootings. He said he didn't think anyone in law enforcement said those vehicles were definitely the getaway ones used by the sniper. "We were trying to find a witness," Bald said. "The media was starved for detail." And the media, he said—not the investigators—had concluded this must be the shooter's vehicle.

On Tuesday afternoon, October 15, Chief Moose and Spotsylvania County Sheriff's Maj. Howard Smith released two FBI-prepared composites of the suspicious white van that witnesses said they saw leaving the Exxon station Friday morning after the shooting there. Two possible models were depicted: a Chevrolet Astro van and a Ford Econovan. Both had ladder racks on top. If anyone was driving one of those vans, Major Smith said, and was in the vicinity of the shooting Friday morning, he or she was requested to call police—immediately. "If you know anybody that drives one of these vehicles that you might suspect," Smith implored, "please call."

It was a scary time to be driving a white van or a white box truck. Ray and Shirley Kirk, grandparents and antiques dealers, had just moved to the small town of Frederica, Delaware, and were driving those exact vehicles. Ray Kirk drove a white Isuzu box truck with black lettering and a dent in the rear bumper. Shirley Kirk had a white Chevrolet Astro van. Scared and suspicious, the Kirks' new neighbors called police, who put the couple under surveillance for a week. In the afternoon, on Monday, October 14, they both left their house, separately driving the two vehicles to ferry goods to a new store they were opening. Ray, fifty-nine, had furniture in the box truck. Shirley, fifty-six, had glassware in the van. They were following each other on a rural back road when suddenly two Delaware State Police cars, lights flashing, zoomed up fast behind them. One trooper pulled over Ray Kirk. The other trooper crept toward Shirley Kirk's van, his gun drawn.

Oh my God, right vehicles, wrong people, Shirley thought.

"Get out of the car with your hands up!" the trooper thundered at her. He yanked her door open, pointed the gun at her head and ordered her to the ground. The trooper's hand was shaking hard, and he was sweating. All of a sudden, more cops came barreling out of the cornfields. Police officers surrounded her husband and his truck.

Shirley Kirk, a size two who has arthritis, was lying on the ground, handcuffed, spread-eagle, being frisked. "I was eating Delaware dirt," she said later. It was so tense, Kirk was thinking the cop would shoot her if she breathed the wrong way. "I was so afraid he was going to kill me," she said. "I was petrified." She was worried about her husband with his bad heart. She wondered: Does he know I'm OK?

"Do you know why you are being apprehended?" an FBI agent barked.

"Yes, the vehicles," said Shirley Kirk. "But we aren't who you think we are."

The troopers and the feds plowed ahead. They

pushed her into the cruiser, searched the van, then wanted to search the couple's house. When the agents walked in, their eyes bulged out of their heads. The place was a shambles, with countless boxes of antiques piled everywhere. The ordeal lasted about four hours. As the last FBI agent was leaving her house, he said, "Well, welcome to Delaware." Months later, Shirley Kirk would say she was grateful for her vigilant neighbors, and even for the hyper police: "They were only doing their jobs."

On Wednesday, October 16, two days after the shooting of Linda Franklin, Tom Manger and his detectives were stymied. So were Chief Moose, Mike Bouchard, Gary Bald and members of the sniper task force in Montgomery County. Eyewitness accounts from the parking garage, police said, were vague and inconsistent. The descriptions were all over the map. Some said he had olive skin. Possibly of Middle Eastern origin. Or maybe Hispanic. "There are a couple of people who believe they saw a man shoot," Montgomery County Police Capt. Nancy Demme told reporters at a press conference. "Unfortunately, because of darkness and distance, and perhaps excitement and adrenaline at the time, we are unable to come up with a composite. We don't have a refined description to go by. I know that's not what the public wants to hear."

During the press conference, Demme offered the members of the public a lesson on what to do if they happened to be near a shooting: Get down and find cover if you hear gunfire. Look in the direction of the sound. Make a mental note of the people or vehicles nearby. Commit what you saw to memory. Write it down on paper or your hand, and don't "contaminate" your memory by comparing observations with other bystanders or reporters. Stay in a safe place until the police arrive.

Demme told reporters that one Home Depot witness was convinced he saw the shooter use an AK-74, a high-powered Russian-made assault rifle able to fire .223-caliber bullets. Keep an open mind, she urged. "The witness firmly believes this is the weapon that he saw," Demme said. "Keep in mind that, just like the vehicle, each witness firmly believes what they do see. It's not to discredit the witness in the least. That may be what he thinks he saw, and we have to keep in mind that weapons are interchangeable, as are vehicles. . . . Please don't narrow your focus to just one weapon."

The Pentagon was getting into the act.

Now the sniper would be chased by secret spy planes. The aircraft were actually called RC-7 Airborne Reconnaissance Lows. They were equipped with special sensors that would help authorities respond to sniper attacks. If there was another attack, the planes' telescopic cameras could be directed toward the shooting site. Defense Secretary Donald Rumsfeld was responding to a request from the FBI. But Gary Bald was steamed that the information about the high-tech Pentagon help was made public. "That was a nightmare," he said. "We were tipping our hand to an investigative tactic."

Before Linda Franklin was shot, the sniper task force had had about a half-dozen suspects under surveillance. The police euphemism was "persons of interest." They had come to the task force's attention through the thousands of tips phoned in to the FBI and local police departments. The names were posted on the big board at the police command center.

After the shooting at the Home Depot, the names came off the board. Surveillance stopped. Task force members began focusing on an entirely new crop of characters. And police officers and agents continued arresting people who illegally possessed guns. Law enforcement had no trouble finding plenty of undesirables. But none was the sniper.

Tom Manger's detectives and patrol officers were putting in twenty-hour days, just like the cops in the other places that had had shootings. Many slept in their offices. Manger lived not far from police headquarters, so some nights he worked until 2 A.M., went home for a nap and a shower, then came back a few hours later. Everything was a blur. One night, having left unusually early, Manger pulled into a gas station around 8 P.M. in usually bustling Tysons Corner, an area of Northern Virginia with acres of congested malls. "It was a ghost town," he said. A cop for twenty-six years, Manger has never been nervous walking down dark streets anywhere. As he pumped his gas that night, however, Manger scanned the horizon, one thought in mind: He wanted to get the heck out of there as fast as possible. "Everyone has a story like that," he said. "It changed the way people lived their lives."

13

A Brief Hiatus

On Thursday, October 17, the sniper task force was dealt a major black eye, a real shiner.

Across the Washington area, residents were increasingly frustrated with the failure of police not only to stop the shootings but also to offer persuasive evidence that they were making progress at all. In schools, the restrictions on outside activity had kids and teachers on edge. Weekend soccer games had been canceled, leaving parents to fill gaping holes in the kids' schedules without straying anywhere near a shopping mall, a highway, anywhere at all, really. It was as if the entire region—more than five million people—were in a bizarre lockdown, and no one could say when it would come to an end.

As horrifying as the shooting of Linda Franklin had been, the eyewitness accounts provided to police afterward seemed to offer some hope that the sniper might be slipping up. He had pushed things too far, ventured away from his trusty shooting places concealed in the woods, and allowed himself to be seen drawing down on Franklin in a busy parking garage. One eyewitness even identified the make of the sniper's rifle, the Russian-made AK-74 assault rifle. Finally, with some hard evidence to go on—instead of the relentless focus on the mysterious white box truck—it seemed like it would be only a matter of time before the phalanx of law enforcement agents pursuing the sniper brought him to bay. Relying on the man's account, Chief Manger and the other officials directing the task force investigation had implored the public over the past forty-eight hours to please be on the lookout for a cream-colored Chevy Astro van with a ladder rack and a malfunctioning taillight. The eyewitness had described the shooter in the parking garage and had even provided a partial tag number from the rear of the van. Newspapers and TV reports ran accounts of the eyewitness's description. It was a bonanza of information!

And all of it was bogus.

It fell to Manger to deliver the news. "Information provided by one of the witnesses at the scene of the shooting in the Home Depot," he told reporters at a packed news conference, ". . . is not credible. In addition, there have been several media reports related to the description of a specific weapon and the suspect. That information, as well, is not reliable."

As much as ordinary residents were shocked and angered by the news—who would make up such a story? why?—no one was more frustrated and angry than Manger and other top police officials. After digesting the account of the eyewitness, they had ordered their troops to put in even longer days than before, running down leads around the clock on every AK-74 that had ever been sold anywhere near the Washington area. Other cops had been dispatched to run new checks on Astro vans purchased far and wide. They checked AK-74 rifle owners who also owned white vans—a list of ten or eleven people, whom officers further investigated. Empty coffee cups piled up. Computers whirred through the night. Bleary-eyed cops catnapped where they could. But they were energized, too. With the kind of description the eyewitness had provided, the sniper's shooting days were surely numbered.

The news deflated many of the cops and federal agents on the sniper task force like a day-old balloon. Manger's detectives had expressed doubt about the man's story from the start. It didn't jibe with accounts that had been provided by other bystanders. Perhaps it was understandable, some thought at first. The lighting in the parking garage was poor. The fear and adrenaline involved in having witnessed a murder, everyone knew, could skew perceptions wildly.

But to make up something like that?

Chief Moose, Mike Bouchard and Gary Bald knew they had a big job on their hands. Cops are like everyone else, only more so. They get up. They get down. But most are the kind of people who don't do the job for the money. The pay isn't great, and the risks can be high. For those who do the job truly because they love it, there are few challenges, few highs, greater than a big, high-profile criminal investigation. They can sustain the high only for so long, however, and a setback like the one dealt by the lies of the eyewitness at Home Depot can really level a blow to morale.

Moose tried as best he could to put the evil genie back in the bottle. Investigators, he said, still had other solid leads. They would be worked and worked hard. "It has not set back the investigation," he said.

Despite the bogus eyewitness account, Moose and the task force leaders said, they were continuing to search for a light-colored van because it had been credibly reported at an earlier shooting, even though it actually hadn't been seen at the Home Depot shooting. Backtracking, in a search for new clues at the Home Depot parking garage, Manger, consulting with Moose, ordered dozens of police cadets to scour the place for evidence. Of course, he was concerned that the site might have been contaminated by foot and vehicle traffic during the three days since the shooting. The cadets searched the garage, then the surrounding area, walking shoulder to shoulder through the grass and pavement on the other side of busy Route 50. "We're just trying to be thorough, trying to be accurate," Moose told reporters. "That's just what investigations are. It is just work, rework, rethink, relook, reinterview, rethink and continue to also stay on the track of moving forward."

Detectives were concerned about widely broadcast images of the AK-74. Focusing on that particular gun, task force officials feared, would lead people to exclude other kinds of weapons. The ATF's Bouchard reminded reporters that the sniper was firing rounds in the .22-caliber family, such as a .221, .222 or .223. The ammunition could be fired by more than thirty different kinds of weapons. Each manufacturer, Bouchard said, had a number of different models, so the actual number of potential weapons they were looking at was significantly higher than thirty. Witnesses, Bouchard said, might be unable to tell the weapons apart. So, he warned reporters, be careful when you are interviewing potential witnesses: "They may not know exactly what kind of gun it is."

Was the sniper a terrorist?

Certainly, according to the definition of Spotsylvania County Sheriff Ronald Knight. But was he a *real* terrorist, in the sense of the September 11 attacks? Was he a member of Osama bin Laden's sprawling international al Qaeda network? As the FBI's Gary Bald had said while fencing with CNN's Wolf Blitzer the previous Sunday, "nothing was being ruled out."

At Bald's request, the question was explored intensively. CIA operatives and U.S. military teams in Afghanistan had placed dozens of suspected al Qaeda operatives in the special U.S. military detention center in Guantánamo Bay, Cuba. The men had been captured during the fighting in Afghanistan, either by American forces or coalition militias like the Northern Alliance. Those deemed to have ties to al Qaeda or the routed Taliban regime that had fled from the capital of Kabul into the rugged Afghan mountains were brought halfway around the world to the sunny if not altogether friendly environs of Guantánamo Bay. There, Pentagon linguists and intelligence officers, coordinating with CIA specialists and FBI agents, debriefed the captives. They had been asked plenty of questions since the start of their detention about Osama bin Laden and the Taliban's messianic Mullah Omar. Now the Muslim men in the open-air prison cells were being queried about an anonymous man with a rifle murdering people in and around

Washington, D.C. Was it part of an al Qaeda plot? Senior law enforcement officials had pretty much dismissed the possibility early on. Terrorists normally will claim responsibility and make some statement of the objective they hope to achieve by resorting to violence. That wasn't the case in the sniper shootings. Questioning the Guantánamo detainees was just another avenue to explore. Like so many others, it didn't really go anywhere.

On Friday, October 18, Fairfax County police arrested Matthew M. Dowdy, a thirty-seven-year-old construction worker, on charges of making a false statement to a law enforcement officer during an investigation. The misdemeanor offense was punishable by up to six months in jail and a one-thousand-dollar fine, and a couple of months later Dowdy would plead no contest, meaning he didn't dispute the evidence but didn't admit guilt either. Commonwealth's Attorney Robert Horan, the top prosecutor in Fairfax County, said that Dowdy wasn't even in the parking garage at the time Linda Franklin had been shot, four days earlier; he had been in the Home Depot, browsing. Turns out he was photographed by the store's security camera. Even Chief Moose made no effort to mask his feelings this time. "I think many people are disgusted," the chief told reporters, "that that happened."

Was Dowdy motivated by the big pot of reward money? Moose cautioned that there was a sturdy system of "checks and balances" that would keep people from receiving the half-million dollars. To make any reasonable claim on that money, the chief said, the information provided had to lead to the arrest or indictment of the sniper.

Reporters pressed another angle. They had tried it on Moose before, but he had refused to rise to the bait. Was the possibility of a link being explored between the sniper shootings and the September 14 shooting at the Silver Spring liquor store? Moose, finally, gave a bit of ground. When the sniper was caught, the chief said, he would certainly be questioned about the Silver Spring incident. "It is an open case. We have not ruled it in and not ruled it out." Behind the scenes, detectives already were looking hard at the case. They believed it was connected.

Late in the day, a vehicle rental agency near Dulles International Airport, in suburban Virginia, called the sniper task force. A cleaning crew had found a shell casing in the rear of a white box truck that had been returned by a rental customer. Police seized the truck immediately. The casing was whisked to the ATF lab in Rockville for testing. It was the wrong size.

The second full week of life with the relentless sniper was ending just as another weekend was about to start. Chief Moose urged residents, once again, to try to go about their lives as normally as possible. "We can't be intimidated as Americans," he said. "Law enforcement is standing up. We're out and about. . . . But we can't be everywhere all the time."

It had been four days since the sniper's last attack—his longest hiatus since the shootings began on October 2. No one wanted more shootings, God knew. But the quiet was unnerving. The sniper seemed to like to take weekends off. But he also, as the shootings of Iran Brown and Linda Franklin showed, had no compunction about changing his plans.

Now that the weekend was here, many worried that the sniper might listen to all the TV talking heads and deviate from his routine again and strike on the weekend. More soccer matches were scuttled. Some youth-league football games were moved out of town. Fall street fairs and festivals were canceled. It was going to be an indoor weekend. Another one.

Heading into the weekend, Chief Moose urged people to look on the bright side. "Any day without violence," he said, "is a good day."

14

"Don't You Know Who You're Dealing With?"

In late afternoon, long before Chief Moose was ready to end his day, his office phone in Montgomery County Police Department headquarters received a series of phone calls.

The first was at 4:23 P.M.

The next came in a burst, just minutes apart.

4:27 P.M.

5:03 P.M.

5:36 P.M.

5:56 P.M.

Like a lot of professional investigators, Gary Bald relies on a few hard-won truths to keep him fixed on the task when things go awry, hot leads turn into dead ends, and solving the crime at hand seems about as likely as winning the Powerball sweepstakes with that one-dollar ticket from the 7-Eleven. Before he was assigned the top job in the FBI's Baltimore field office, Bald had been detailed from his post as the number two man in the Atlanta office and sent to Boston to direct what would turn out to be one of the most sensitive investigations in the FBI's history—a probe of the FBI itself, or, rather, of the handling of a controversial Mafia turncoat named James "Whitey" Bulger. Bald's investigation would consume forty-five months. By the time it was over, Bulger's former FBI handler, retired agent John J. Connolly Jr., wound up serving a lengthy prison term and the Bureau had—despite a desperate attempt by officials in Boston to sweep the scandal under the rug—cleaned house thoroughly and convincingly.

Patience, his colleagues said, was one of Bald's long suits. Bald, discussing the sniper investigation, put it another way. "I felt confident," he said, "that we had the information [we needed] to solve the case. It's just like dropping a puzzle out on a table. . . . If you've got that one piece, it helps you put the rest of the pieces together."

Bald had no way of knowing it at the time the phone began ringing off the hook in Chief Moose's office that Friday afternoon, but a number of pieces of the puzzle were about to start coming together.

Three days earlier, almost to the minute before the first of the calls to Chief Moose's office phone, at 4:35 P.M. on Tuesday, October 15, a dispatcher at the Rockville Police Department received a call from a pay phone in Woodbridge, Virginia, a suburb more than thirty miles away.

"Don't say anything—just listen," the caller said.

The man was agitated, talking fast. "We're the people causing the killing in your area. Look on the tarot card. It says 'Call me God. Do not release to the press.' We have called you three times before trying to set up negotiations. We've gotten no response. People have died."

The dispatcher tried to steer him elsewhere. "I need to refer you to the Montgomery County hotline." The caller had phoned the number for the police department of Rockville, a municipality within Montgomery County that had no involvement in the sniper investigation. "We are not investigating the crime," the dispatcher said. "Would you like the number?"

The caller hung up.

On Thursday, October 17, the Montgomery County Police Department received two calls. The first, like the errant call on Tuesday to the Rockville Police Department, was logged at exactly 4:35 P.M. The second was received at 5:40 P.M. Both calls went into the line for the public information officer, who typically handles calls from reporters.

Sgt. Derek Baliles picked up the receiver. The man on the other end of the line was a mess, pumping coins into the pay phone. "I am God!" the man roared. "Don't you know who you're dealing with? Just check out the murder-robbery in Montgomery if you don't believe me!"

Baliles listened, confused. There had been no murder-robbery in the county recently. Just the sniper shootings, and none of those involved robbery. Next, the caller rambled on about a Sergeant Martino. The name didn't mean a thing to Baliles. Was the caller just another nut, a crackpot impelled to get into the act by the endless sniper news?

Baliles waited for more, but there was none.
The line went dead.

It was almost a given that William J. Sorukas Jr. would go into law enforcement. His father, William J. Sorukas, had retired from the Indiana State Police as a first sergeant detective. Then he went to work as a criminal investigator with the Indiana Department of Revenue—altogether some thirty-seven years in law enforcement behind his shield. The younger Sorukas, known to friends and colleagues as Billy, was a burly forty-two-year-old with sandy hair, a major in criminology and, like his dad, a fondness for pursuing bad guys. A police officer for the state of Indiana until May 1986, Sorukas decided to see a bit of the world and joined the U.S. Marshals Service, starting out in San Diego, where he quickly rose through the ranks to become coordinator of the fugitive group for the San Diego violent crime task force. His group bagged more than seven thousand fugitive felons.

Created in 1789, the Marshals Service is the nation's oldest law enforcement agency, responsible for everything from protecting federal judges and jurors to providing security and new identities for criminals who have either had a change of heart or for other reasons decided to apply for membership benefits of the Federal Witness Protection Program.

Hunting fugitives, however, is what Sorukas loved most. Over the years, he had worked on other big cases: spree killer Andrew Cunanan, who crisscrossed the nation before killing fashion designer Gianni Versace in Miami Beach; railroad serial killer Angel Maturino Resendiz; the Texas Seven prison escapees;

and Clayton Lee Waagner, charged in 2001 with mailing anthrax hoax letters to women's clinics.

In the sniper case, Sorukas and the Marshals Service would employ an investigative tactic never tried before. They can't reveal many details about it because they don't want to give criminals an edge. But they started out examining literally millions of records of phone calls around each shooting, for half an hour before and after each one, looking for any cell phone numbers that turned up more than once. That work meant contacting wireless phone companies immediately after a shooting occurred. The marshals worked through a little-known group called the Wireless Emergency Response Team. This is a consortium of wireless companies, law enforcement, and other emergency government agencies. The WERT was formed on the night of September 11, 2001. Working side by side with traditional emergency rescuers, the WERT's purpose then was to use wireless technology to analyze cell phone signals from the debris at Ground Zero at the World Trade Center to try to find possible survivors. The WERT investigators were unable to find any survivors at Ground Zero, but they realized how valuable such an organization could be in future crises.

Working with the team meant Sorukas and the marshals could place just one phone call to WERT, provide a password, and WERT would instantly contact the cell phone companies. It all had to be done superquickly, however. Five minutes after a shooting was too late. The shooter could be miles and miles away by then.

No one knew if the sniper even had a cell phone,

but like disseminating the composites of the white vans and box trucks, it was a long shot investigators had to try. Soon, Sorukas's investigators saw a handful of numbers popping up over and over at shooting sites. A quick investigation revealed a dead end: They were the cell phones of task force investigators. But there were some benefits. Using the new technology, the marshals could tell different police departments when it was unlikely their top suspects were the sniper. Sometimes, the marshals were able to rule out a top suspect completely. Not that the information was always exactly welcome, of course. Some police departments were unconvinced by the wireless sleuths. Prince William County, for instance, had been eyeing a pair of brothers, one of whom had been fired from an Ohio police department. He's not the sniper, the marshals told local police there. The police even had one of the brothers under surveillance at a location far from the Home Depot the night Linda Franklin was shot, but the cops still believed the man might be the sniper. Sometimes, it was tough letting go of a seemingly good suspect.

Poring over the voluminous telephone records, it would take time to discern a pattern, to sort wheat from chaff.

By Saturday, October 19, however, Billy Sorukas and the marshals had learned about the call to Derek Baliles, the public information officer for the Montgomery County Police Department. The marshals geared up. They got records of hundreds of phone calls to that same line for the past several days, focusing only on calls made from pay phones. If it was really the sniper who made the call, they'd look at pay phones first, eliminating calls made with phone cards or from residential phones. Hours later, the marshals traced the call to Baliles back to a pay phone in Ashland, Virginia.

Then they looked at incoming and outgoing calls from the same phone for five hours before and after the Baliles call—a complicated task that took hours. Like a lot of the investigators in the case, some of the marshals were working until 3:00 or 4:00 each morning, catching naps on a sofa in the office. Sleep was no big deal anymore.

They weren't there yet, but a pattern would soon emerge. Whoever was calling police, if he really was the sniper, was sloppy but not altogether stupid. The first call had been misdirected, to the Rockville city police department. The next was closer to the mark, to Derek Baliles, in the public information office of the Montgomery County police department. Right department, wrong guy. But even here there was a clue. The caller had mentioned a murder-robbery in Montgomery. He also had mentioned a Sergeant Martino. There was no one by that name with that rank in Chief Moose's department. Eventually, they would learn there was a Sergeant Martino in another Montgomery police department, and that was in Montgomery, Alabama. Last was the series of calls made directly to Moose's office.

The caller had every right to feel as though he had finally sorted through the communications jumble and, finally, gotten straight to the source, the man directing the sniper investigation. The only problem was, Moose's office was in chaos. His harried, normally even-tempered secretary, often assisted by a sergeant, was fielding over two hundred calls a day. On most, she could do no more than place callers on hold and try to get back to them to take a message. Only calls from numbers or officials she recognized immediately, like Gary Bald or Mike Bouchard, would be put through to the chief directly.

The snipers, clearly, wanted to talk.

But they had created such a maelstrom of chaos and confusion they were simply unable to make the connection.

Other connections were being made, however, slowly, laboriously. And though neither the snipers nor the law enforcement posse pursuing them could know it yet, a clock had suddenly begun ticking.

15

"I Am God"

The snipers made at least one more call that Friday afternoon.

The calls to Chief Moose's office had been made from pay phones in rural Ashland, Virginia, about ninety miles south of Washington. Tooling around the pleasant town with its quaint antiques shops on a warm fall afternoon, the middle-aged man and the teenage youth in the battered Caprice were frustrated. They couldn't get through to police.

Perhaps someone else would listen.

At the town's YMCA, staffers gave the man and his young companion the phone number of a priest at St. Ann's Roman Catholic Church. The man and the boy decided to place a call.

Sitting in the church rectory, Monsignor William Sullivan listened closely. Very briefly, there was the voice of an older man. "Here, someone wants to talk to you," he told the priest. He then quickly handed the receiver to someone much younger. That person was ranting. The priest could barely understand him. It was the younger of the two who did most of the talking. He had a peculiar accent, but the priest was unable to place it.

"I am God," the younger caller said. He repeated the phrase several times, ordering the priest to write his words down and communicate them to the police. Write this down! If the police didn't believe what he was saying, the caller told the priest, they should check out a shooting near St. Ann Street in Montgomery. Then he paused. *Alabama,* the caller added.

The priest thought the call was a crank.

Billy Sorukas and his team of marshals had a ton of phone calls to sort through, but as fast as they were and even with the new information they had to help them cull the most promising, the task was still enormous.

The FBI's Rapid Start system provided an organized triage system for calls coming in to the police hotlines, but by Saturday, October 19, the FBI's tip line alone had received tens of thousands of calls. There was just no way to get through that number of calls quickly and still pay careful attention to their content. The work was tedious, mind-numbing. But there was no way around it. It had to be done.

One of the calls that had come in toward the end of the week seemed to merit another look, but it didn't get put in the "urgent" file right away. At 5 P.M. on Thursday, October 17, Robert Holmes had phoned the FBI tip line from his home in Tacoma, Washington. He didn't know for sure, he said, but his former army buddy, John Williams, might be behind the sniper shootings. Holmes had served with Williams at Fort Lewis, Washington, and he had seen his friend just three months earlier in Tacoma with a black male he referred to as his "son." The youth, Holmes guessed, was about eighteen, and Williams had christened him with a nickname: "Sniper." Williams, Holmes said, had an M-16 rifle with a scope and had gone through a bitter divorce from his wife and lost custody of his three kids. Williams, he said, also goes by the name John Allen Muhammad.

Why did Holmes think Williams might be in the Washington area?

Holmes wasn't sure, but he thought Williams might be traveling from Washington State to Florida. Also, his wife had apparently moved with the kids to the Washington, D.C., area to get away from Williams.

The call was logged on a Rapid Start lead sheet. Someone would get around to taking a look at it as soon as time permitted.

There is literally no way of measuring, much less codifying in any logical order, all of the information stored away in the computer databases of all of the nation's various government agencies. There are, however, with a few key data points, ways for determined and savvy investigators to begin to put together files on individuals they decide they need to learn more about. It's not just cops who need to know the tricks to make the computers sing. Child-welfare investigators, securities regulators, insurance examiners—all must deal with so much computerized information that knowing the tools, and having the patience, to help cut through all the data are often the difference between success and failure and, occasionally, life and death.

In the case of forty-one-year-old John Allen Muhammad and seventeen-year-old Lee Malvo, it would take several more days and a few lucky breaks before investigators knew where to focus their efforts. Once they did, however, they would find the data pickings rich and the story they revealed unusual in the extreme.

Back on December 19, 2001, some ten months earlier, INS Border Patrol agents in Bellingham, Washington, had detained both Una James and her son, Lee Malvo, after determining they had entered the country illegally. They were fingerprinted and handed over to INS.

That record would provide an early data point for investigators.

There would be more.

Lee Malvo and Una James were sent to INS facilities—she to one in Seattle, he to a juvenile center near Spokane. But because neither one had a criminal history, the INS released them on January 23 pending a deportation hearing, scheduled for November 2002.

After the sniper arrests, the U.S. Border Patrol and the INS would quarrel over whether Malvo and his mother should have been deported immediately and whether they should have been released before the deportation hearing. It was a bureaucratic squabble, of little interest to the sniper's pursuers, although they certainly wondered how things would have turned out if Malvo been deported immediately.

The details of Malvo's life after he came to the

United States and moved to Bellingham, Washington, would provide further data points and help explain the genesis of the young man's relationship with John Muhammad. But that picture, too, would take time to develop.

John Muhammad had moved to Bellingham in the summer of 2001 after he returned to the United States from Antigua with the three kids he had with Mildred. He wrote in court documents that he returned from Antigua because the island "seemed pretty backward—no Internet or other technological advances." So, he showed up on August 16 with the kids at the Lighthouse Mission, a Christian homeless shelter on a hillside overlooking Puget Sound. The three-story stucco building with a large cross out front is located in a gritty, industrial section of Bellingham, a small, quiet town of sloping hills and fir trees populated by retirees, hippies, college students and fishermen who seek its clean air and laid-back, outdoorsy pace. Bellingham is about one hundred twenty miles north of Tacoma and twenty miles from the Canadian border. When he showed up at the mission doorstep, Muhammad was looking for a place to live with the kids. It was not completely unheard of that a parent would arrive with children in tow.

The three children—John, Salena and Taalibah—were "neat, clean and lovable," says the Reverend Al Archer, who ran the place and got to know Muhammad during those fall months. Muhammad was a very clean-cut man who dressed well—not in finery but in good clothes that weren't ripped or tattered. "He always looked neat, no matter how he was dressed," Archer said. "He was soft-spoken and his manners were impeccable. It was 'Yes sir,' 'No sir,' 'Could I help you?' He always seemed glad to help out. I never saw him seem angry or anything like that. He was too good to be true."

Muhammad enrolled the three kids in Parkview Elementary and Whatcom Middle and looked for help from other agencies. "He was doing everything right," Archer said. "He seemed to really care about the children, and the children seemed to love him." At times, the children playfully climbed all over their dad. "The only times I saw him laugh or appear to have fun was when the children were climbing on him."

All that changed on August 31, however, when Whatcom County sheriff's detective Tom McCarthy found the children enrolled under fictitious names at school. He took them away and placed them in protective custody. At the mission, Muhammad did not make a scene. He simply maintained that he was supposed to have the children and that this was all the result of a big misunderstanding.

That was when Archer began to doubt that Muhammad really was too good to be true. "When this perfectly nice gentleman had his children taken away from him," he said, "I realized we were dealing with a dishonest person and that he was not Mr. Clean."

The real blow, though, came a few days later during a brief hearing in a courtroom of the Pierce County Courthouse in Tacoma. That hearing, on September 4, 2001, may well have led to Muhammad's undoing. During the proceeding, Mildred Muhammad was granted full custody of the three children and the right to leave the state without telling him where she was going. John Muhammad represented himself but was stunned by the judge's decision. He seemed devastated, repeatedly asking if that meant he couldn't see his children.

After the hearing, Mildred Muhammad disappeared with the children, secretly moving across the country to live with relatives in their townhouse on Quiet Brook Lane in Clinton, Maryland, in suburban Washington, D.C.

Muhammad was optimistic he would get the kids back. A month later, on October 5, he stopped by the Opportunity Council to see if they could help him locate housing. On his application, he listed his three children, adding that they weren't in school yet because they were waiting for paperwork from the Caribbean. "I'm currently at the Lighthouse Mission and homeless and have no work and need help," he wrote on his application. "I have my family with me."

The court records of that custody dispute, the divorce case, even eventually his housing application all would yield more data points for investigators. But they, too, would take time to unearth.

At the time Malvo was detained by the INS Border Patrol agents, he was John Muhammad's closest companion. In October, several months earlier, Malvo had run away from his mother, who worked at a Red Lobster restaurant on Florida's southwest coast. Somehow, he had made his way from Florida to Washington, where he went to live with Muhammad at the Lighthouse Mission in Bellingham. To any who asked, Muhammad introduced Malvo as his son.

After making a good first impression at the mission when he had moved there with his three children from his marriage to Mildred, John Muhammad had begun to alarm at least a few people there. He stood out at the Lighthouse Mission. He wasn't your typical homeless man. Mission manager Rory Reublin said Muhammad always seemed to have money, wore nice clothing, and talked about his travels to Jamaica, New Orleans and Texas. He never gave staffers a reason for all the traveling and said he paid for it by doing odd jobs. Still, it was highly unusual for a person in a homeless shelter to be jetting around and getting phone calls from travel agents. "I had a gut feeling about him that something wasn't right," says Reublin, who himself lived in the streets for a couple of years. "I just had a feeling that this guy was more than he was appearing to be, but never did I think what it turned out to be."

Muhammad would be gone on various weekends and later tell mission staffers he had been traveling cross-country. Both Reublin and the Reverend Archer were worried. Archer wondered where Muhammad was getting money for plane tickets. "It didn't add up," said Archer. "We thought he was up to something, but we didn't know what it was." It was not long after the 9/11 terrorist attacks, and Archer thought seriously about calling the FBI because he thought Muhammad might have been "working with some organization making plans to do harm to our country. He fit the pattern of what we were reading about." Archer said that Muhammad never made any comments supporting the terrorist attacks while he stayed at the mission.

After Muhammad lost his children in the custody dispute with Mildred, he had asked Archer to write a letter of recommendation for him in his bid to regain them. Archer agreed, but had to leave for a short vacation before he could finish the letter. Away from

Bellingham, he was troubled by Muhammad's increasingly odd behavior. Nevertheless, he called the mission and asked a staff member to e-mail him the letter so he could finish it. The staffer warned him against doing so: "I don't think you want to write that letter." Archer agreed and decided to call the FBI, which he did while still on vacation. "I told people," he said, "that someday you'll read about him in the newspapers."

The warning, unspecific as it was, resulted in no action. But it would become another data point in the dossier the sniper task force investigators eventually compiled on Muhammad and Malvo.

Malvo's presence at the mission, when the Reverend Archer returned from his vacation on October 22, 2001, was another source of unease. Archer first saw the young man sitting in the chapel with Muhammad. "I didn't believe Lee was his son," Archer said. "I believe he had just somehow come to know Lee and had pulled him into going with him."

To others at the mission, Malvo was quiet, neat, cooperative. Obviously smart and well-mannered, he was, Archer said, "just like John. He never caused any kind of stir or objected to anything. He got along with everybody." But—and it was a big but: "Our staff," Archer said, "had the feeling that he [Malvo] was being pulled along by John into something really too big for him."

The relationship, to many, appeared unusual. In the evenings at the mission, Muhammad and Malvo sat and talked intently, but their interaction was subdued. "They were always huddled together, talking," said Reublin, the mission's manager. "They were always apart from everyone else. I can't remember

Lee Malvo ever talking to anyone else." Once, they were spotted reading the Bible together. At night, they slept on big, thick mattresses on the carpeted floor of the cafeteria, where staffers sometimes put people when the mission was crowded.

Malvo entered Bellingham High School, where classmates described him as a well-mannered, well-dressed, conscientious student who offered to tutor other teens. But school officials were concerned that they had no records of his previous schooling.

When Malvo wasn't in school, he worked out with Muhammad at the Bellingham YMCA, sometimes daily. The two came in together, shot baskets and swam laps.

The older man and his younger companion had their regular haunts. Night after night, Muhammad and Malvo would frequent Stuart's Coffee House, a neo-hippie hangout where they would hunker down at the same table, drinking coffee and playing chess, sometimes until midnight, well past when the mission had closed its doors. They were regulars but didn't really talk to other patrons there. "It was like the younger one was a student," said Hannah Parks, who sang and played guitar at Stuart's. "He was very respectful of the older one. He seemed to look up to him." On some late nights, the two were spotted wandering around downtown. "They seemed somewhat normal," said Parks. "They didn't seem homeless or strange."

Muhammad took an interest in Parks's eldest boy, age four, whose father was black. He asked Parks, a white single mom, if she was going to talk to him about his cultural background. He also told Parks that he was a music producer who could help her career.

He told her he was going to the East Coast and that he knew people in the music industry and asked her if she wanted to come. No thanks, she told him. "I found out he was staying at the mission, and I didn't know what to think," she said. She noticed that Muhammad always carried a green duffel bag, so heavy it strained him to carry it. She had no idea what he was keeping in the bag, but he took it everywhere, even into the bathroom. He also carried a lot of money and offered to buy her drinks and food. "I didn't think he was dangerous," she said. "He didn't ever act angry. He was nice and polite. He didn't seem weird."

Around the mission, Muhammad was very protective of Malvo and would not allow him to speak to other adults who lived there. Mission manager Reublin said that during dinner one evening, Malvo got his plate, sat down at the table first and began talking with the other residents at the table. Then Muhammad sat down and glared at Malvo across the table. "Muhammad gave him a stern look, a look telling you to be quiet," Reublin recalled. "He shut up immediately, like someone put a cork in his mouth. He just looked down and ate." It struck Reublin that Muhammad had extremely strong control over the boy. He said he never talked about religion with Muhammad but noticed that before meals Muhammad and Malvo would pray with their hands out. They attended a church play together in early December as well as the required nightly chapel service. "They would listen and never were disrespectful or disruptive," Reublin said.

There was a stretch when Muhammad and Malvo ate lunch daily at the Community Food Co-Op. They usually shelled out about six or seven dollars each time, paying cash or using an electronic food stamp card. James Fritzinger, who worked in the co-op's café, chatted with Muhammad, mostly about cooking, a subject the older man appeared to know quite a lot about. Muhammad always was helping Malvo, whom Fritzinger took to be Muhammad's son, with his studies. Once Fritzinger overheard him telling the youth, "You will end up in jail if you are stupid."

16

Pieces of a Portrait

There was another picture of John Muhammad emerging among some who knew him in Bellingham, and it was not quite so benign.

Some, in fact, thought it scary.

Harjeet Singh had befriended Muhammad and Malvo during a YMCA workout, then invited them over to his house a few times, and met them at the co-op for lunch and tea. Once, Muhammad confided to Singh that he was a converted Muslim and made several anti-American comments. The downfall of America had already begun, Muhammad added, with the attacks on the World Trade Center and the Pentagon. Singh begged to differ. Many of his countrymen had worked in the World Trade Center and had perished there. The attacks, he told Muhammad, had taken many innocent lives. Muhammad kept mum. He had made his point.

In the weeks to come, investigators would learn of

other anti-American comments Muhammad had made during his rambles around Bellingham. One morning not long after the September 11 attacks, Muhammad was nursing a beer at the Waterfront Tavern, a bar open from 6 A.M. to 2 A.M. on Holly Street, in the gritty industrial section of town, just blocks from the Lighthouse Mission. He started telling Loren Martinson, a salmon fisherman turned construction worker, that the United States was the real terrorist in the world today, going around the world killing people who disagreed with it. It was time, Muhammad said, that America got a taste of its own medicine.

You better watch what you're saying, Martinson told him. "You are the wrong color, for starters. And you are staying at the Lighthouse Mission. You aren't in too good shape to be saying what you are saying."

Muhammad nodded silently. He wasn't belligerent.

Later that afternoon, Muhammad strolled into The Horseshoe Cafe, a working-class, fishermen's hangout, a Bellingham fixture for more than a century. The place features a saloon called the Ranch Room with a big, long bar and a large Western mural, painted about forty years ago, hanging behind the bar.

Planes were still grounded, and everyone still numb. Wearing jeans and a green army-type jacket, Muhammad sat on a barstool and ordered a beer. The Horseshoe's regulars were all watching television news coverage of the terrorist attacks in New York and at the Pentagon.

"Let's nuke them sons of bitches," roared Drew Sandilands, a crab fisherman whose cousin was the pilot on the second plane that crashed into the World Trade Center. "Let's kick their asses."

Muhammad was a few stools away. He didn't say anything for a few minutes. Then he started making anti-American comments. He had served in the military, he said. He knew how America treated people overseas. "We're the terrorist state," he said. "We're the ones who are the terrorists in the world."

Sandilands nearly erupted. His buddies at the bar had to hold him back. "You think that way, you better get over to Afghanistan with the rest of those sons of bitches," the fit fisherman said. "Or else I'm going to use you for crab bait."

Martinson, the construction worker, moved to stop Sandilands from punching Muhammad. "It's not worth it," he said. "I wouldn't waste my time."

Martinson ordered Muhammad to leave.

Sandilands turned around and Muhammad was gone. "He ducked out real quick," Sandilands recalled. The fisherman ran outside to see what kind of car Muhammad was getting into, but the man was nowhere to be found. When Sandilands came back to the bar, he told his friends they had better watch out for that guy. "Hey, he kinda fits the profile of a terrorist. He's a perfect example."

Martinson sauntered back down to the Waterfront Tavern a while later and found Muhammad. He bought him a beer and proffered some advice. "You don't run around talking to people you don't know saying stuff like that."

"Yeah, you're right," Muhammad agreed.

"See you later." Martinson took his leave.

Months later, Martinson recalled the man making the incendiary remarks but said "he didn't seem like a wild man."

Muhammad, wisely, never returned to the Horseshoe. In the mornings, he hung out at the Waterfront Tavern, which features a few beat-up pool tables, some darts and a jukebox. For about four months, Muhammad came in every morning around 7:00— just after the mission opened for the day. He always took the third barstool from the end, sipped a Bud or two and watched the news on Channel 7. He kept to himself and eventually wandered up the street to hit a few more pubs, places like The Cabin, where he knocked back some more draft Buds. "He was very nice and polite," said Millie Ulmer, the Waterfront's bartender. She kept her distance, however, and a sharp eye on him. "There was something about him that didn't seem right," Ulmer said "You know how you get that feeling about someone."

In the coming weeks, as they began piecing together the broken shards of John Muhammad's personal and professional life, investigators would learn more about him, finding other bits of data and hearing about other people's encounters with him, enough to draw something of a portrait.

While he lived at the Lighthouse Mission, Muhammad picked up extra cash doing odd jobs. Donald Haaland had been the maintenance man at Country Garden Apartments, an apartment complex in Sumas, Washington, a sleepy town minutes from the Canadian border. Haaland couldn't do all the work around the complex. So he would recruit day laborers at the mission. In August 2001, he needed help with a roofing project at an apartment building. He met Muhammad at the mission and found him to be quite friendly, "very concerned" about his personal health and in very good physical shape. Haaland later told police that he used to pick Muhammad up at the mission every day because he had no transportation and that he worked for him until November 2001. Haaland told police that he never saw any firearms on Muhammad but said that Muhammad did mention once that he had a gun he wanted to put a silencer on. The gun, Muhammad told Haaland, was for someone else. Try H and H Sporting Goods on Dupont Street, Haaland suggested; the place was just a short walk from the mission.

Real-estate agent Greg Grant and his wife, Elizabeth, had owned the Country Garden Apartments for a little more than four years. Muhammad was such an outstanding worker that Grant kept going back to the mission to get him for jobs, such as pulling weeds, fixing gutters, repairing the roof. Muhammad worked at the apartment complex maybe twenty times over several months. Every time he worked there he always greeted Grant respectfully: "Good morning, Mr. Grant." He was safety conscious, taking pains, for instance, to make sure the ladder was placed safely while working. Grant said Muhammad was the best worker he'd ever had from the mission. "He worked out really, really well," said Grant. "He did everything in a very clean and professional manner. He was nice to the tenants."

Grant was puzzled, though, about why such a smooth, polished, well-groomed man was living in a homeless shelter. "I'm going through a divorce," Muhammad told him. "I'm trying to put my life back together. I'm trying to get custody of my kids." Muhammad made up another story, though. He told Grant that he was a teacher and that he had five kids (though he neglected to add with three different mothers). But Grant had the impression that Muhammad was sincerely trying to get his life in order. "It all made sense. Going through a divorce is difficult," Grant said. "It looked like his direction was to get his life back on track. He seemed like a parent who wanted his kids back."

On a couple of occasions, Muhammad brought a youth with him whom he introduced as his son. "There was a bond between those two," Grant said. "This appeared to be a loving relationship. John seemed like a caring, devoted parent." The boy would sit in an open spot at the apartment complex and read a book while Muhammad worked. When Grant would ask why the boy wasn't in school, there was always a plausible explanation, such as students had the day off because teachers had a professional meeting.

But there were times when red flags went up. A couple of times, Grant said, Muhammad would say he wasn't going to be around on a particular weekend. "Where are you heading?" Grant asked him. Muhammad was headed to Miami, he told Grant, to catch a plane to an island—Grant recalls it was either Jamaica or Bermuda—because he needed to sign some papers.

"What do you mean?" Grant asked.

Muhammad was selling his house, he explained.

"That's what FedEx is for," Grant said. It all struck Grant as odd because he knew real-estate transactions weren't normally conducted on weekends. Even more, he wondered: How can a guy living in a mission afford to be flying to the Caribbean? Still, Grant thought perhaps there was an explanation for it. He's going through a divorce, he has a house, Grant thought, maybe there's some money there for him.

He's trying to get his life in order. It made sense to Grant, though, even if it was still a bit odd.

Grant was by no means the only one puzzled by Muhammad.

Kristine Sagor was the on-site manager at the Country Garden Apartments. She was just plain spooked by Muhammad. He had done excellent work, but she found him "very manipulative" because he was trying to get her to ask him to move in with her. Instead, his claims about his past alarmed her and she found him slippery. She said Muhammad was an "exceptionally fit" man obsessed with physical conditioning. He told her he was forty-eight years old. Muhammad sometimes talked about fasting for days on end and claimed to have spent twenty years in the Special Forces—but wouldn't provide any details. He also told her that he had spent fifteen years selling commodities, but when she confronted him about the years not adding up, he was elusive. When he told her that he recently had gone to Jamaica with his son for the weekend to sign some papers about a house he was selling, she challenged him again. Why was he living in a homeless mission if he could afford plane tickets to Jamaica? Again, he was elusive.

One day, Muhammad asked Sagor for a ride to a house on South Beach Way. Sagor later told police she took her dog for a walk along the beach while Muhammad talked to a man there. According to police reports, she said when she returned, she could hear them talking about shortening the barrel of a gun, making a collapsible stock and getting a silencer. He later told her that he hadn't wanted to go to a gun shop that required a lot of paperwork. He also said he wanted to buy the rifle for his son so they could go shooting together, adding that he already had a similar rifle of his own.

The other man was Glen Chapman. He operated a small gun shop out of his home. Chapman hadn't remembered the man's name, but he later told police that the man asked him if he could cut down the barrel of a Winchester Model 70 rifle. He said he wanted the barrel threaded so the gun could be broken down and carried in a case. He told Chapman that he wanted the gun for his son who lived in a southern state, noting that he wanted his son to be able to carry the rifle when he went to the shooting range.

Chapman was so concerned that he contacted the ATF. Muhammad's request was downright strange. If his son were stopped by police with that kind of weapon, he would be clapped into jail in a heartbeat. Chapman had told Muhammad that what he wanted done would be very difficult. He wasn't interested in doing the job under the circumstances. According to police reports, Muhammad never asked about a silencer, Chapman said, and if he had, he would have ordered him to leave his property. The whole thing was so bizarre, Chapman wondered briefly if Muhammad might be an undercover ATF agent trying to get him to do illegal modifications to guns.

Kristine Sagor was also unnerved. On November 30, 2001, she contacted Bellingham High School to tell them about the modified rifle intended for Lee Malvo. Like Chapman, she too tried to call the ATF, and she also spoke to Bellingham police officer Jeffrey Hinds. Sagor was afraid of Muhammad, she told Hinds. If Muhammad knew she had given authorities the information about Malvo and the rifle, she added, she believed he would come after her and retaliate.

Sagor's calls triggered a chain of events that ultimately led authorities straight back to Lee Malvo. In trying to figure out who he was, they would learn he was in the country illegally. And that, in turn, would point to his detention on December 19 and his release a month later and the pending deportation hearing. It was a chain of events leading to the possibility that Muhammad would lose Malvo through deportation, a huge blow after the loss of his three children.

More pieces were coming together.

After Sagor's call, Hinds checked with Bellingham High School. There, administrators informed him that Malvo was living with his father at the Lighthouse Mission. The school had no information beyond that. Muhammad had told school administrators that Malvo had attended a private school in Jamaica the year before and had earned the credits of a senior. School administrators told Hinds that the transcript to back up the claim looked suspicious. They hadn't been able to confirm the information with any school in Jamaica.

Hinds continued his inquiries. By December 6, he had obtained a set of Malvo's transcripts from Jamaica and Fort Myers. They listed Una James and an Antoine Eveque as the young man's parents. A Florida health form also listed Antoine Eveque as a parent. No documents provided a Social Security number for Malvo. And there was nothing in any of the paperwork about a John Muhammad. The records were a muddle. Hinds sought help from the detective bureau. Looking for a way to make some connection that made sense, Detective Allan Jensen ran the names of Malvo, Muhammad, James and Eveque through the police records of Fort Myers and Lee County, the Florida county where Fort Myers is located.

Nothing.

But that wasn't the end of the trail. On December 10, Bellingham police detective Allan Jensen learned about the custody dispute back in August, when Muhammad's three children had been taken away from him. A check of the court records revealed no mention of a sixteen-year-old boy. Now the detectives were stumped. Who was Lee Malvo? Who was John Muhammad?

Bellingham officers checked to see if Muhammad was in the country illegally. Nope. Muhammad had been detained for twenty-four hours by agents of the Immigration and Naturalization Service when he entered the country in April 2001, but had refused to answer any questions. Eventually, the INS agents determined that Muhammad was a U.S. citizen. The immigration file revealed that Muhammad appeared to be in good physical health; his mental health, however, was questionable, the file said. And the INS had nothing on Lee Malvo at that point.

Friday, December 14, 2001, was a gray, gloomy day.

Lee Malvo's mother, Una James, had called the Reverend Al Archer at the Lighthouse Mission. She was worried and upset. After a long trip by Greyhound from Fort Myers, Florida, to Bellingham, she was exhausted. But she had come, James told Archer, to find and reclaim her son. He had run off to Bellingham to live with John Muhammad in the Lighthouse Mission.

James was distraught and worried. She didn't want her son to have anything to do with John Muhammad.

Archer jumped into his van and met James at the bus station. He didn't want her coming to the mission, where she could run into Muhammad and Malvo. James had traveled all the way across the country with boxes of her possessions. The mission director was impressed by her seriousness of purpose. "I saw a mother who came to try her best," he said, "to get her son away from someone he shouldn't be with."

Archer bought James dinner at a restaurant near the mission. Afterward, he helped her get a motel room. Before she checked in, however, they drove around Bellingham, talking about different options for wresting Malvo from Muhammad. Archer suggested calling the police and explaining the situation—"that her son had left home and that he is with this older person and that she wants him back with her."

It sounded like a plan.

At the police station, James told officer Keith Johnson that she had had several phone conversations with Malvo since he had run away from Florida in mid-October. The calls had come from two places, according to her caller ID. One was the Lighthouse Mission. The other was a Tacoma address James believed belonged to one of Muhammad's relatives. James told Johnson that she had not reported her son as a runaway to the Fort Myers police because she had hoped to talk him into coming home without getting the police involved.

Around 7 P.M., two officers pulled up to the Lighthouse Mission to get Malvo. Just as they were getting out of their car, the officers spotted the boy and Muhammad walking out the front door. Malvo told officer Kent Poortinga that he had come to Bellingham from Fort Myers because it was "as far west as I can go." He told the cop he wanted to get away from his mother's bothering him and to get a better education, which he thought he was getting at Bellingham High. Malvo said he thought there were better opportunities in Washington. He told the officer that he had met Muhammad while eating dinner at the mission. He said that since he was a teenager, Muhammad had offered to help him out by calling him son around the mission and getting him enrolled in school.

It was, at best, an implausible tale.

The two officers decided to check it out. Without incident, they escorted Malvo to the police station, where his mother was waiting. "He was not too pleased to see her there," Reverend Archer recalled. After considerable discussion, the police officers determined that Malvo could not be turned over to James until she reclaimed her identification. Her documents were stuck on a Greyhound bus in Chicago, but she knew they would get to Bellingham the next day. Malvo was sent to a foster home for the night. James's papers did arrive in Bellingham on another Greyhound the following day, and she was able to get her son released into her custody. By then, out of Muhammad's presence for nearly twenty-four hours, Malvo's attitude had visibly softened toward his mother. "He was more happy to be with her," Archer recalled. "There was some mom-and-teenage-son joking and friendliness." James and her son went back and stayed at the mission for a couple of nights.

On Tuesday morning, December 18, however, Officer Hinds discovered that Malvo was back at Bellingham High. He was surprised. He thought the boy would be going back to Florida. Detective Jensen and Hinds met with Malvo at the school that morning. What was going on? they asked. Why was he there? Wasn't he going back to Florida?

Malvo was polite and cooperative. After he was released to his mother, he told the officers, he had persuaded her to allow him to finish high school in Bellingham. After graduation, Malvo said, he planned to attend Western Washington University. His mother had agreed to all this, Malvo told the officers, and had allowed him to return to the Lighthouse Mission. Malvo repeated his explanation for why he had come all the way from Florida to Bellingham. It was the farthest point he could find from Fort Myers. He had never liked the feel of things in Florida and had come to Washington State for change.

It was quite a yarn for a sixteen-year-old, the officers thought. Then they asked about Muhammad.

Malvo, once again, had a ready answer. Yes, he said, he knew John Muhammad from around the mission, but that was it. He really had had very little contact with the man. He and Muhammad were friends, Malvo continued, but it was more a relationship of convenience. Muhammad had agreed to act as his father for the purposes of school registration.

How was he getting by? the cops asked Malvo. Where did he get his money?

His mother had been wiring him one hundred ninety-two dollars every two weeks via Western Union,

Malvo replied. Another ready answer. He used the cash for food, clothing and school supplies, he said.

And why had his mother relented, allowing him to remain in Bellingham?

James had come to Washington to get him, Malvo said, because she had been concerned that he had not been calling her often enough in Florida. When they were first reunited, after his night in the foster home while James waited for her identification papers, Malvo said, his mother told him she planned to take him to New York City, where she intended to enroll him in a fashion design school. Malvo hated the idea, he told the police officers, and his mother had finally agreed that he could stay behind in Bellingham and finish his high school studies there.

The officers asked Malvo more about his past. How had he come to live in the United States?

Malvo related a long, complicated tale. He had lived in Antigua for a few years with an aunt after graduating from school, he said, then quickly corrected himself. He had *not* graduated from high school but *primary school*. He left Antigua when he was in the eleventh grade, Malvo continued, and used his Jamaican passport with the U.S. visa stamp in it to move to America to live with his mother, who was already in Florida. He had since lost his passport, Malvo said, adding that when he had entered the United States, in Miami, his mother picked him up.

The two police officers were openly skeptical. Malvo's story about his mother wanting to take him to New York, they said, flatly contradicted what Una James had told them about their plans to return to Florida.

Malvo persisted. Their plans had changed, he said,

after he and his mother talked together. The plan now was for him to stay in Bellingham.

Talk about a puzzle! Malvo was quick on his feet, his answers well thought out, Detective Jensen thought. But his dates and times for things were all tangled up. There were too many inconsistencies. Something was fishy. The detective decided to do some checking.

A call to the Border Patrol was in order, Jensen thought. The questions about Malvo's relationship with his mother and with Muhammad—those might take some time to sort out. But there was an obvious legal question. Malvo said he had lost his passport, so there was no way of telling if he really was who he said he was, no way to confirm the details of his story about entering the United States. Heck, there was no way to ascertain what country he was even from.

Border Patrol agent Keith Olson listened to the account of Malvo's story from Jensen. Olson knew he needed to check it out.

The next day, he and agent Raymond Ruiz picked up Malvo and his mother.

Border Patrol agents fingerprinted Malvo and, following procedure, entered the prints into the agency's vast computerized database. The record, at the time, was just one more tiny blip in the vast sea of data the federal government maintains in its computers.

When investigators from the sniper task force came looking for it, however, this was one data point that would light up the night. In Gary Bald's formulation, the Malvo fingerprint would be that "one piece of the puzzle" that let you start putting the other pieces together.

* * *

With the detention of Lee Malvo—and the threat of deportation hanging over the youth—John Muhammad was suddenly threatened with the loss of the only person in the world with whom he still had any kind of close personal relationship. Muhammad had already lost his three children with Mildred, not to mention his older son, Lindbergh, from his first marriage. Nor did he have much of a relationship with his eldest son, Travis, from an earlier relationship.

Some of those closest to Muhammad say they detected a big change in him back in January. Months earlier, Muhammad was being represented by attorney John Mills in his bid to win back custody of the three children from Mildred. When he first met Muhammad, Mills told the *New York Times,* he saw him as "an ordinary, unassuming guy" who merely wanted his kids back. In the months since, however, Mills thought, Muhammad had "melted down."

How and why, and whether that had pushed him to lead his teenage companion on an unprecedented killing spree nearly three thousand miles way—those were questions the investigators would have to start piecing together.

17

"Word Is Bond"

Saturday, October 19, seemed a slow day. The sniper hadn't struck in five days. The FBI's Gary Bald took a little break that afternoon, left the Montgomery County police headquarters and went to the Powerboat Show in the quaint, waterfront town of Annapolis, Maryland. He had been so consumed by the case that this was the first time he had a little downtime. At the show, Bald even bumped into his media guy, Barry Maddox. It was good to be away from the case, even for just a few hours.

But when Bald got home that evening, his pager was going off: Shooting in Ashland, Virginia.

Stuart Cook had just showered and was settling into his favorite chair with a Stuart Woods mystery when the phone rang. The fifty-nine-year-old sheriff of Hanover County, Virginia, had spent the day puttering around the house, but his mind was elsewhere.

Like other police departments across the region, Sheriff Cook and his officers had made plans for what he called a terrible "what if." But so far they had been lucky. Last year, he hadn't recorded a single homicide in his county of nearly ninety thousand people.

The sheriff dearly wanted to keep it that way.

The phone at his side rang, and Cook picked it up immediately: A man had been shot over at the Ponderosa steak house.

Cook's heart sank.

He threw down his book, put on his uniform and raced to the restaurant. The sniper's five-day vacation, evidently, was over.

Jeffrey and Stephanie Hopper lived in Melbourne, Florida, and were planning to visit an ill relative in Pennsylvania. A friend urged them not to drive through the D.C. area: "Just don't get out of the car." The Hoppers wrestled with the decision but decided to go.

They were on their way home when they pulled off Interstate 95 for gas and dinner. They left the steak house at 7:59 P.M. and were walking toward their car. Stephanie Hopper, a Boeing engineer assigned to NASA, heard a sound but didn't recognize it as gunfire. Witnesses said later the shot had come from the woods along the parking lot's edge.

"I've been shot," Jeffrey Hopper said, falling to the pavement.

The single round struck Hopper in the abdomen, then splintered into shards, ripping his stomach, severing his pancreas, grazing a kidney and traveling up to his chest. Hopper was rushed to Medical College of Virginia Hospitals in Richmond, in critical condition. He went through three hours of surgery that night and a second operation Sunday evening, during which doctors removed a small piece of lead. The evidence was rushed to the ATF's crime lab in Rockville.

A deeply religious man who also writes and sings country music, thirty-seven-year-old Hopper would eventually be released, but not before he underwent five surgeries and spent a full month in the hospital. As a result of the shooting, he lost his spleen, part of his pancreas, and two-thirds of his stomach, as well as some sixty-five pounds. His doctors said Hopper faced a long recovery.

No one knew if the attack was the handiwork of the sniper; ballistics confirmation wouldn't come until Monday. But no one was taking any chances either. "We're going to treat it as if it is until we know it's not," Sheriff Cook, a lifelong resident of the Richmond area, told reporters.

The FBI special agent in charge in Richmond, Virginia, Don Thompson was at a restaurant when his text pager said, "Call the office." He rang his office and learned about the shooting, hopped into his car, leaving his wife with their friends at the restaurant. From the south side of Richmond, he got there in about thirty-five minutes.

Law enforcement officials had devised a strategy in advance, and it fell into place right away. That meant another massive dragnet, with officers shutting down long stretches of Interstate 95, the East Coast's major corridor. Once again, helicopters circled overhead. State troopers and sheriff's deputies searched cars one by one, even though no one knew exactly who they were looking for. In Virginia, police blocked every exit of the Interstate from Richmond to north of Washington, D.C. Police officers manned entry-

ways into the District of Columbia from Virginia and
Maryland. Traffic was halted at the American Legion
Bridge between Maryland and Virginia. Police also
threw up checkpoints on many other primary roads.
They were looking for white vans with one or two
people inside. At the same time, officers jotted down
the license plate numbers of every vehicle at every
fast-food place, business and motel within a mile of
the shooting.

But they couldn't find him.

Again, there was a report of a white van seen near
the shooting. A sheriff's deputy pulled one over on an
entrance to I-95 but soon let the driver go. After interviewing witnesses, the police declined to put out a
lookout for any particular vehicle.

Any good cop wants to be where the action is.
That's what they sign up for. But that's exactly what
top law enforcement officials in Richmond, such as
Sheriff Cook and the FBI's Thompson, did not want.
They formed a perimeter around the crime scene and
limited access. They didn't want dozens of cops inundating the crime scene. Still, more than two hundred
fifty officers were there to help out, some combing
the woods, parking lots and streets, hunting for bits of
evidence. It had rained lightly, and officers and federal agents inspected a muddy field and a construction site for possible tire tracks and footprints. At 6:30
the next morning they were back—time for a grid
search.

Ashland is a tranquil, rural town with little more
than six thousand residents. It bills itself as "The Center of the Universe" on its official town Web page.
Located in central Virginia about fifteen miles north
of Richmond, Ashland was born in the late 1840s as

a railroad resort town and developed into a small college town, home of Randolph-Macon College, a liberal arts school of one thousand one hundred students. People gravitate to Ashland for its historic Victorian homes, antiques shops, stately maples and oaks. But it's the town's gentler, slower pace that people especially want. That the shootings had moved so far away from Washington, D.C., unnerved not only the Richmond area but also the entire region. It was as if no place were safe anymore.

The Ponderosa is located on a commercial strip of fast-food places, motels and gas stations, a few blocks from the Interstate. Detectives rapped on doors at motels along the roadway, waking people up. Had anyone seen any suspicious guests? What about a white box truck or white van?

Nobody, once again, had seen anything.

At 9:40 A.M. Sunday, October 20, the sniper called the FBI tip line and directed police to carefully inspect the woods near the Ponderosa. There, he said, they would find a note.

Investigators had already discovered it the night before. The note was four pages long and had been placed in a plastic bag tacked to a tree outside the restaurant. A local investigator and an FBI agent jumped on a state police helicopter bound for the FBI lab in Washington. There, the note was opened in the wee hours of the morning. Technicians processed it, checking for fingerprints, possible fibers and DNA evidence. Was there any sweat, blood, saliva, skin or hair on the note? The lab sent a copy of the note back to Hanover County. It was there by 8:30 Sunday morning.

The snipers had given a 6 A.M. deadline for when they would contact police. But the FBI techs were handling the evidence with care so they didn't contaminate any DNA evidence. So, the cops missed the deadline. The handwriting would be compared with the writing on the tarot card, the examination conducted by the U.S. Secret Service Crime Laboratory's Questioned Document Branch. The conclusion? Both, almost certainly, had been penned by the same hand.

The neat, block printing on the first page of the note was surrounded by five stars. Not surprisingly, the whole thing was riddled with spelling and punctuation errors:

> For you mr. Police
> "Call me God"
> Do not release to the
>   Press.

> For you Mr. Police
> "Call me God."
> Do not release to the press.
> We have tried to contact you
> to start negotiation. But the
> incompitence of your forces in
> (i) Montgomery Police "Officer Derick"
> at 240-773-5000 Friday.
> (ii) Rockville Police Dept. "female officer"
> at 301-309-3100.
> (iii) Task force "FBI" "female"
> at 1 888-324-9800 (four times)
> (iv) Priest at ashland.
> (v) CNN Washington D.C. at 202-898-7900
> These people took of calls

for a Hoax or Joke, so your
failure to respond has cost
you five lives.
If stopping the killing is
more important than catching us
now, then you will accept our
demand which are non-nego-
tiable.
(i) You will place ten million
dollar in Bank of america
account no. 4024-0046-2875
-9173
Pin no. 9595
Activation date 08/01/01/
Exp. date 09/04
Name: Jill Lynn Farell
Member since 1974.
Platinum Visa Account.
We will have unlimited ~~withdra~~
Withdrawal at any atm world-
wide.
You will activate the bank
Account, credit card, and pin
number.
We will contact you at
(Ashland, VA)
Ponderosa Buffet tel #798-9205
6:00 a.m. Sunday Morning.
You have until 9:00 a.m.
Monday morning to complete
transaction.
"Try to catch us withdrawing
at least you will have less
body bags."

(BUT)

(ii) If trying to catch us now
more important then prepare
you body bags.
If we give you our word
that is what takes place
"Word is Bond."

P.S. your children are not
safe anywhere at any time.

Not surprisingly, given their other miscues, the snipers had written down the wrong phone number for the Ponderosa. It was one digit off. The Ponderosa number was 804-798-8205—not 9205 as the sniper had written.

The FBI quickly set up a system to forward telephone calls that came in to both the incorrect and correct numbers to the FBI negotiations team at the command center in Montgomery County. They didn't know which number the snipers might use, and they wanted to be ready for both. But it was a nightmare for the negotiators, too, because the Ponderosa phone line was deluged with phone calls after the shooting, especially from reporters. So those calls rolled over to the FBI negotiation teams, too.

Later that morning, task force investigators met Monsignor William Sullivan at the door of St. Ann's in Ashland. The priest was about to say Mass. The sniper, the investigators said, could well be a member of the priest's parish. Sullivan calmly conducted the service, then sat down afterward to tell the investigators in detail of the strange call he had received on Friday. There had been two callers, an older and a younger man. He tried to describe the younger caller's accent but still was unable to place it. The younger man had boasted about a killing near St. Ann Street in Montgomery, Alabama. Investigators thanked Sullivan for his time. Then they quickly took their leave. The Alabama lead was a live one.

They needed to jump on it—quickly.

At 3 P.M., an officer with the Henrico County Police Department, near Richmond, saw a 1990 Chevrolet Caprice with New Jersey tags on the road ahead of him. That car looks strange, the officer thought, so he ran the license plate number. The Caprice had been pulled over six other times that month, and every time, its tags were clean.

The Caprice went on its way.

At 4:53 P.M., the Virginia State Police ran another check on the Caprice in Glen Allen, Virginia, also near Richmond. Same story. The car wasn't wanted in connection with any crimes. There had been no police lookout on it. The owner wasn't wanted for any crimes that the cops knew about.

No red flags. The Caprice vanished again.

18

Gold-Plated Leads

Billy Sorukas had worked straight through the weekend.

By Sunday afternoon, October 20, he and his team of marshals were confident the sniper was nearly within their grasp. They had figured out that over the past several days, the shooter had made nearly a dozen calls from pay telephones in and around Ashland, Virginia. Many of the phones were outside convenience stores up and down England Street, where the Ponderosa was located. Sorukas plotted all the sites on a big map that had the locations of all of the shootings since October 2.

There were other pieces of the puzzle. Derek Baliles, the Montgomery County Police Department information officer who had fielded a call from the sniper, described him as having a peculiar accent, one he was unable to place. In Ashland, Monsignor Sullivan had said the same thing—only he said there had been two callers, and it was the one with the younger-sounding voice who had the accent. Sullivan, too, had been unable to place its origin. Investigators checked surveillance cameras near the stores where the pay phones were located. Maybe, just maybe, whoever made the calls had gone inside to get change for the phones. And maybe, with a bit of luck, the caller might have walked near a camera on the way into or out of the store. There were plenty of people on the reams of film examined by the investigators, but nothing indicating anyone was the person who had made the calls identifying himself as God.

Despite the frustration, Sorukas felt things were beginning to come together. The calls were gold-plated leads. So was the note left at the Ponderosa with its chilling demand for ten million dollars and the postscript—an obscene afterthought, almost—that the area's kids were not safe.

Sorukas focused on the calls. A young man with an accent phones the public information officer at Chief Moose's department, rants and rambles about a shooting in Montgomery. Same thing with the priest—only this time, he says, in effect, "Oh, yeah, by the way, if the cops don't believe me, tell 'em that's Montgomery, *Alabama,* near St. Ann Street." Plus, with the priest, there were two callers, handing the phone off to each other. Then there was the burst of calls to Moose's own office Friday afternoon, all from Ashland pay phones the day before the Ponderosa shooting.

"These are the guys," Sorukas thought.

In a lot of big, complex, fast-moving investigations—and the sniper case was one of the biggest—detectives spend hours checking out leads and suspects that fizzle out. There are always dead ends, way too many. It's slow, frustrating work. But in every case, when the puzzle pieces start fitting together, things move fast. Very fast.

Late Sunday afternoon, things started moving fast. Sorukas spoke to an ATF agent at the command post in Montgomery County. "Is anyone looking at the information from the pastor?" Sorukas asked. "We need to see what's going on down there."

We're all over it, the ATF agent guaranteed. Monsignor Sullivan had been debriefed by task force investigators after he said Mass earlier in the day. We're pursuing this one hard.

Sorukas thanked the man and hung up.

The task force had other important leads, he knew, and they were pursuing those as well. One of the best was the credit card number they had used in the note demanding the ten million dollars. A quick check showed the card had been stolen in Arizona back in March. It had also been used on April 9 in Tacoma, Washington, to pay for twelve dollars and one cent's worth of gasoline. Two more leads, both gold-plated.

On Sunday evening, Virginia police met with school district officials in the Richmond region. It wasn't the kind of meeting any of the police executives had ever imagined having. The police had sobering information. The sniper, they warned, might deliberately target children. The police didn't share details about the note and made no reference to the possibility that there might be more than one sniper. They did make it clear, however, that the information was not for public consumption; they merely wanted to provide the best guidance they could to school officials, consistent with their law enforcement obligations.

Mark Edwards was on the spot. He was the school superintendent for Henrico County, where Richmond is located. That's the neighboring county to the one where the sniper had left the note at the Ponderosa. He was also the father of two daughters, one in high school, the other in middle school. Both girls attended county-run schools. What was the right thing to do, not just for his kids but for all the kids that had been placed in his care? No one had ever experienced anything like this before. The sniper, Edwards and the other school district leaders knew, had already attacked and seriously wounded a child, thirteen-year-old Iran Brown. But for the fast thinking of his courageous aunt, young Iran would almost doubtless be dead. "The potential was there for our children to be in the line of fire," Edwards said. No one wanted to surrender to the sniper and allow fear to rule his life. At the same time, no one wanted to take any chances. In the end, prudence prevailed.

School officials unanimously decided to close schools in four districts in the Richmond area the following day. It was a drastic step affecting at least one hundred and forty thousand kids. The plan was that schools would reopen Tuesday but would be on lockdown, meaning no outdoor and evening activities. There would be only one entry point at each school, increased police patrols. Football games would be postponed.

The sniper, once again, was directing events.

At 7 P.M. sharp, a tight-lipped, sober-faced Chief Moose approached the podium at the police command center in Rockville. The day before, he had told reporters there would be no press conferences Sunday. The shooting of Jeffrey Hopper outside the Ponderosa restaurant had changed that.

"We'll take no questions on no topic," Moose said evenly. "And we just ask you to understand."

The chief's message was brief. First, he thanked Hanover County Sheriff Stuart Cook for his department's quick response to the shooting Saturday night. Then, Moose appealed directly to the assembled reporters and camera crews. Please, he said, convey this next point as directly as possible. "Carry it clearly," he said, "and carry it often.

"To the person who left us a message at the Ponderosa last night, you gave us a telephone number. We do want to talk to you. Call us at the number you provided."

It was the first direct message from the police to the sniper, an unusual, high-stakes appeal to a killer. Let's talk.

But how to find the right words for such a dialogue? With Mike Bouchard and Gary Bald, Chief Moose had spent considerable time pondering the question. He had plenty of resources to draw on, but in the end, as Bald pointed out, there's no script. "No one teaches you how to do that," Bald said. The FBI could supply all kinds of support. Its Critical Incident Response Group was on call. Round-the-clock experts in crisis management, crisis negotiations, tactical operations and behavioral assessment were an easy phone call away. But "there's no manual that tells you what to do," Bald said weeks later. "When I was standing behind the podium, there were no easy answers. There's no class you take."

Bald himself had plenty of training in dealing with the media, especially in high-profile corruption, kidnapping and extortion cases. Still, it's hard to think of another case where literally hundreds of reporters were being asked to convey a message to a killer. How do you control something like that? "Anytime we deal with the media," Bald said, "we think in terms of 'everything we tell you could compromise a prosecution or investigation.'"

But there was no alternative. The snipers had reached out to their pursuers, first through phone calls, then through the note left outside the Ponderosa. The police *had* to reply. In addition, Moose, Bald and Bouchard knew that getting the killer talking was perhaps the best way to catch him. Moose, as the public face of the police effort to apprehend the snipers, had to also be the voice of the investigation. As he concluded his appeal, reporters scribbled frantically in their notebooks. To them, it wasn't entirely clear what the sniper had said in his note; the news was that he had made an overture to police.

In that, Moose, Bald and the other leaders of the sniper investigation hoped that perhaps the public would see evidence of something they had so far been unable to demonstrate very much of—progress. If the sniper was willing to talk to police, maybe there was reason to think that the shootings would stop, that he would turn himself in. If that was too hopeful, Bald thought, perhaps the families across the region who had been so traumatized by the continuing spasm of violence would draw some other comfort from Moose's remarks: The investigators weren't going away. They weren't giving up. They were going to work this investigation until the gunman responsible for the spree of murders was brought to justice. "People needed to hear from the people responsible for the case," Bald said. "If the shootings had stopped, we wouldn't have just disappeared."

Around 8 P.M., John Wilson got a call from Maj. Pat Downing.

The gregarious chief of police in Montgomery, Alabama, Wilson had spent the weekend with his brother, James, a sergeant over at the police department in Gwinnett County, Georgia. The two had taken in the Atlanta Falcons–Carolina Panthers game earlier in the day, cheering their beloved Falcons to a 30–0 rout before celebrating with a dinner at the Outback Steakhouse. Chief Wilson had the salmon because he was on a diet, and a weigh-in was fast approaching. Back at his brother's house, he was settling in to watch a bit more football when he was roused by the phone.

"I know this will sound really far-fetched," said Downing, Wilson's chief of detectives. "But I've gotten a call from a detective with the sniper task force in Washington, D.C. He said they had gotten a call from someone professing to be the sniper who said, 'If you don't believe me, call Montgomery, Alabama, and ask them about a murder-robbery near St. Ann Street.' "

The location immediately rang bells for both Wilson and Downing. St. Ann Street was near the Alabama Liquor Control store. Back on September 21, Claudine Parker, fifty-two, had been shot and killed and Kellie Adams, twenty-four, badly wounded as they were locking up the store.

Downing wanted the chief's permission to let a

local FBI agent hand-carry the fingerprint and bullet fragments recovered from the shooting to Washington on Monday. Do it, the chief ordered. The shootings had been one of the most senseless in his jurisdiction, and it preyed on Wilson's mind. "Let's don't get our hopes up," he cautioned Downing. A Montgomery native who had been at the helm of his city's police department for seventeen years, Wilson had seen plenty of promising leads end up as no more than a flash in the pan. "We don't know if this guy is really the sniper."

The chief had good reason to be skeptical. What the professed sniper had said in his call was simply information that had already been in the local press. A lot of reward money was at stake. And the department had received other boastful calls claiming responsibility for the shooting.

Wilson hung up with his chief of detectives. Then, the two Wilson brothers had a long talk—cop talk. Football could wait. Suddenly, a light went off in the chief's head. He remembered the kind of firearms catalog the suspect had dropped during the chase after the liquor store shooting.

He rang Downing back immediately.

"You remember what we found was an accessories catalog for an assault rifle?" the chief asked.

Downing did indeed.

Maybe this was a bona fide lead after all.

19

Identified

At 3 A.M. Monday, October 21, Lenny DePaul was jawboning.

A supervisory inspector U.S. marshal from a special fugitive-hunting task force based in New York and New Jersey, DePaul communicated with the distinctive if not quite dulcet tones of a Brooklyn native, an accent that would be next to impossible to miss at a good thirty paces.

The task force to which DePaul was assigned was an elite unit, its existence specially mandated by Congress. Its job, quite simply, was to hunt the most dangerous, violent felony fugitives—identify them, track them down and put them behind bars. Like a lot of federal law enforcement units, DePaul's team had descended on the Washington area to help Chief Moose's sniper task force, and the other task forces popping up in Virginia—run down leads, sift evidence, sit on surveillance, whatever was needed.

With still a few more hours until dawn, DePaul and the detectives and agents on his team were camped in the lobby of the suburban motel they had managed to find in Virginia. They hadn't slept for four nights straight, but no one felt like going up to his room. Tomorrow would be another long day, and a bit of shut-eye was probably a good idea. Or at least a shower and a shave would have helped. But DePaul, who had thirteen years in with the marshals, couldn't stop working the case. He was one of the few who had seen a copy of the note the sniper left outside the Ponderosa. He had also been allowed to listen in on the phone call the sniper had made to the Rockville municipal police department. Like a lot of calls made to police lines, that one had been automatically tape-recorded. The news from the call to Monsignor Sullivan had also been disseminated to DePaul and his team, as well as to the members of the sniper task force and the many agencies assisting in the investigation: possibly two snipers, not one.

In the motel lobby, DePaul and his guys chewed it all over.

Chasing fugitives, you got all kinds, from all points of the compass—Russian mafia, Peruvian and Colombian cartel members, Jamaican criminal posses. It was a veritable United Nations of criminals. As it happened, two members of DePaul's task force—detective Joe Thomas and officer Vinny Senzamici—*were* experts on the Jamaican crime gangs. A dozen or more of the island nation's violent posses were deep into the illegal drug trade along the Washington–New York corridor, and it was the rare U.S. attorney on the East Coast who didn't have an outstanding arrest warrant on one Jamaican gang member or another.

The taped voice on the call to the Rockville dispatcher intrigued DePaul. "This is a young, black kid," he told his guys. "What was the kid's accent?" he wondered aloud.

"Could it be Jamaican?" an officer asked.

"Very possibly," DePaul said. "Somewhere in the islands."

The two Jamaican-gang experts jumped in immediately. Some of the sniper's references in the Ponderosa note, they said, could be of Jamaican origin. "Word is Bond," for example. The words could be from a song. But which one? And was it really Jamaican? Exhausted, the men fired up their laptop computers. While the others stretched and yawned, the two police officers hunted and pecked. One of the laptops finally spat something out. The rap group House of Pain had a song. The opening words were:

Word Is Bond. Pop pop pop pop
Grab your chest. Now ya bleeding (punk).

It was a song, an anthem almost, about a shooting. DePaul asked for a printout. "What else?" he asked.

The cover page to the Ponderosa note also had five stars on it. Maybe, the Jamaican-gang experts suggested, there was a clue here, too. A drug posse based in the New York area was called the Five Star Generals. Gang members fancied leaving calling cards with five stars on them. A clue?

It was all just theory, DePaul knew, one of the hundreds floating around. But it was a lead. Something else to be looked at.

At 7:57 A.M., someone called the Ponderosa number.

The call was routed immediately to the FBI negotiations team at the Montgomery County command post.

The call lasted thirty-eight seconds. It was jumbled, the words hard to decipher. He instructed police to listen and repeated the "Call me God" introduction. He reminded the FBI negotiator that their terms were nonnegotiable and repeated the threat to children.

At 8:20 A.M., the FBI negotiators passed the call on to a marshal there at the command center. The marshals scrambled, trying to trace the phone the caller had used. The number came back to a pay phone at an Exxon station on busy West Broad Street in Glen Allen, Virginia, near Richmond. That wasn't far from Ashland, the snipers' last-known location. Local police and federal agents were alerted immediately. A battalion hustled over to the gas station through the morning rush hour.

It was raining lightly when the receptionist at the Royal Oldsmobile dealership in Glen Allen glanced outside. It's normally pretty quiet there on a Monday morning. Today, however, there were half a dozen unmarked police cars out front. There were also several marked units. "You better come up here and see what's going on," the receptionist told coworkers.

A small group watched through the dealership's front window. Then someone opened the front door.

"Stay inside the building," a cop boomed.

A SWAT team pulled on its bulletproof vests. "Oh my God, what's going on?" service manager Don Neilson mumbled to himself. He and his coworkers saw the cops pointing at a pay phone at the Exxon station across the street.

A white van was parked there.

"No way," Neilson muttered. "This can't be happening." It was like a war game or a computer game, he thought, but it was all too real. The cops—dressed in black from head to toe, even wearing black boots—were crouched down. More cops peered through binoculars.

Across the street at the Exxon, a white Plymouth Voyager van was parked next to the pay phone. Sitting in the van, the driver was talking on the phone with the receiver through the window. Another man was crossing the street, walking toward the gas station.

Around 8:35 A.M., the SWAT team, guns drawn, descended on the van in just twenty seconds. A SWAT officer who looked like a ninja warrior yanked the van's door open. The others kept their rifles trained on the clearly alarmed man inside. Within three seconds, he was on the ground. Minutes later, nearly two dozen officers swarmed the Exxon station. More rushed in behind them and grabbed the other guy. In the parking lot, the receiver dangled from the pay phone, and TV news crews beat the clouds overhead to froth.

At the Olds dealership, Don Neilson felt a surge of anxiety, but also a sense of relief. Was the sniper siege finally over? And was it happening before their very eyes?

Shortly after 10 A.M., as local and cable TV channels played and replayed film of the arrests at the Exxon station, Chief Moose appeared before more

TV cameras back at the Montgomery County Police Department.

"The message that needs to be delivered is that we are going to respond to a message that we have received," the chief said. "We will respond later. We are preparing our response at this time."

Authorities in Richmond convened a midday press conference. Until just a few days ago, the capital of the commonwealth had considered itself blissfully beyond the sniper's killing radius. Now, as the fleet of television satellite trucks and the mob of reporters attested, it had become a critical locus of the investigation.

Stuart Cook, the Hanover County sheriff who had raced to the scene of the shooting at the Ponderosa restaurant two nights earlier, addressed the impatient crowd of journalists. "The two people we have in custody are being questioned," he said, stating the obvious to an immediately frustrated press corps, "in regards to the sniper shootings."

That was it. The sheriff declined to characterize the two men at the Exxon station as suspects. But across the region, panicked residents were buoyed. Could these men possibly be the snipers? Could the terror finally be over?

The answer was no. Richmond authorities announced hours later that the two men had been questioned, then turned over for processing to the Immigration and Naturalization Service. The men had been in the wrong place at the wrong time. Both were in the country illegally, one from Mexico, the other from Guatemala. More than likely, they would be deported. The day's soaring hopes were deflated.

* * *

Unseen in the dramatic television coverage—and unknown by all but a few on the sniper task force—was this fact: The investigators who descended on the Exxon station had missed the snipers by just minutes, maybe less than half an hour. The snipers had used another pay phone that morning, one located in a different corner of the Exxon station lot. By the time police got there, however, they were gone.

For Moose and his team, the question now was, had the snipers watched the failed police stakeout at the Exxon station on television? If they had, would that damage the trust Moose had been trying to build between himself and the shooters? Would the sniper continue to communicate with the police if he had seen their awkward attempt to catch him? Or would he simply respond by taking another life?

Late in the day, Margaret Faulkner made a call she hadn't truly ever expected to make. An FBI agent based in Montgomery, Alabama, Faulkner had flown from Alabama to Washington, D.C., earlier in the day with a package. It was the fingerprint recovered from the gun catalog dropped by a suspect running from the liquor store after the September 21 shooting there. FBI supervisory Special Agent George Layton's colleagues had picked her up at the airport and whisked her straight to the lab at headquarters.

Montgomery, Alabama, Police Chief John Wilson had urged caution in making premature judgments about the possibility of a link between the shooting in his jurisdiction and the sniper attacks in the Washington area. But FBI technicians had run the print lifted from the gun catalog through the Bureau's vast fingerprint database and gotten a hit.

"They came up with a name," Faulkner told the chief.

Wilson asked a few questions.

The fingerprint belonged to someone named Lee Boyd Malvo, Faulkner said.

Wilson thanked the agent and hung up.

The name Malvo meant nothing to him.

Still later in the day, an ATF agent called Billy Sorukas. "This is what's going on with Alabama," the agent said. "It's good information."

In the FBI computers, Malvo was identified as federal criminal No. 596094VB9. Malvo wasn't actually a criminal per se. His fingerprint was in the FBI database because he had been detained by the INS in Bellingham, Washington, back in December 2001.

Like a lot of cops, Sorukas is a low-key guy not given to elation, but he was pleased. Once we can put a name on someone, we can find someone, he thought. This is what we do best.

Immediately, he redirected his team of marshals: "I know you are working on other things, but I want to know *everything* about Malvo."

It was time to go data-point hunting.

Not long after 4 P.M., a sober-faced Chief Moose appeared before the cameras again. It was his third time since Sunday evening to use the television airwaves to communicate with a killer.

"The person you called could not hear everything you said," Moose said. "The audio was unclear, and we want to get it right. Call us back so that we can clearly understand."

The chief seemed to be referring to the garbled Monday morning call from the sniper. If there was a made-for-TV-moment in the sniper investigation, this was surely one of them, the stern police chief appealing to a killer or killers to reach out and make contact one more time. The cameras lapped it up. In a case fraught with so many dead ends and disappointments, however, the extraordinary dialogue was essential. Moose was careful not to provide any details about the prior call from the sniper.

Just please, he implored, give us another chance to talk to you.

The phone lines to Bellingham began lighting up.

Task force investigators started with the INS office there. That was the first data point, after all. They soon found more. From the Bellingham police department, the task force members learned of Malvo's mother and her visit to the Lighthouse Mission to try to track down her son. The young man had been living in the homeless shelter but attending Bellingham High School, the investigators learned.

Next, the name of John Muhammad popped up. In all the reports, Lee Malvo was said to be keeping company with an older man named John Muhammad.

To Billy Sorukas, poring over the information, it was a fit. Monsignor Sullivan had said there was an older man on the phone before the younger man with the accent went into his "I am God" rant.

Sorukas began working the phones frantically. "We need photos," he said. The INS had detained

John Muhammad at the Miami airport in April 2001. But there were no photos of him. There were, however, photos of Malvo from Bellingham.

By early Tuesday morning, Sorukas had them. He e-mailed them immediately to an FBI agent in Richmond, then had hard copies delivered to the task force command center in Rockville.

Sorukas started putting together a timeline. The focus would be John Muhammad. The mystery man of Bellingham would be a mystery man no longer. With a name and enough other information, Sorukas and his team would vacuum up every government record that ever bore Muhammad's name. Veterans Affairs records, immigration documents—nothing would be overlooked. Nothing could be, now.

20

The Final Shooting

At 5:56 A.M., on Tuesday, October 22, the sniper
struck again.

It was still dark outside, and Conrad Johnson was
just beginning his day behind the wheel of Montgomery County's Ride-On bus Route 34. He was
stopped at Grand Pre Road near Connecticut Avenue
in the Aspen Hill area, near Silver Spring, Maryland, a
layover area where drivers downed a quick a cup of
coffee as they geared up for their morning routes. It's
a spot where a lot of the drivers liked to tidy up their
buses, do their paperwork and plan their routes. Johnson was supposed to roll up to his first stop in a
minute. He was standing on the top step of his idling
bus with the doors open when he was hit—the bullet
rifling neatly through the narrow space between the
doors and hitting him in the upper stomach.

Conrad Johnson, thirty-five, known to some friends
as "CeeJay" and others as "Rad," was born in Kingston,

Jamaica. He had moved to Maryland when he was ten, joining his mother and other relatives already there. Close to his mother, two half sisters, and a younger half brother, Johnson graduated from High Point High School in Beltsville, Maryland. With his wife, Denise—on her most recent birthday, Johnson had gotten all the passengers on his bus to sing "Happy Birthday" to her into his cell phone—Johnson had two sons, Dante, fourteen, and DeVohn, six. Johnson coached Dante's basketball team and loved playing touch football with the boys, dancing in the end zone like a big kid. He wanted his sons to experience all of life. On a visit to New York, Johnson insisted on taking the subway, telling his cousin, "I want my boys to experience everything I did growing up."

Corny as it might have sounded, Conrad Johnson loved the passengers on his bus. In ten years behind the wheel, he had a faithful following of riders, especially senior citizens who often had no one else to talk to. His older passengers baked cakes and Jamaican favorites and brought them to Johnson. "If he was off and someone else drove his run, they would always ask, 'Where's Conrad?' " said a friend and fellow bus driver, Nelvin Ransome. "He was always pleasant."

On cold mornings, Johnson let students waiting at a school bus stop nearby warm up inside his bus. "He greeted people with style," said a cousin, Howard Henry. "Just being in people's lives brought joy to his life."

Conrad Johnson was a big man—six feet, three inches tall and two hundred thirty-five pounds. But he had a reassuring smile and a gentle soul. He had a passion for basketball, loved hip-hop and reggae music, and was always the one to organize summer cookouts, fish fries or cabaret parties. "Everyone knew he had a kind heart," said Ransome. "You'd be proud to say he was your friend."

The shot that felled Johnson seemed to have come from Northgate Park. It was a small patch of woods across from the bus staging area.

Shortly before 6 A.M., Juan Tilleria was on the balcony of his apartment about two blocks away, having his morning coffee and cigarette before heading off to his construction job. When he heard the shot, he nearly dropped his cigarette. Oh, maybe the sniper is striking again, he thought. He went inside, flipped on the TV and waited for the news.

The sniper was back.

After nearly three weeks of murder, mayhem and terror the likes of which most Americans had never experienced before, he had returned to the very place where he had begun his killing spree, making people feel even more anxious.

And still he got away. A witness told police she saw a masked man dressed in black, and holding something like a rifle, get up from a squat and run toward a grassy common area into an apartment complex. Police searched, in vain. Paramedics airlifted Johnson to nearby Suburban Hospital. Doctors tried valiantly to save him, but the .223-caliber slug had done far too much damage.

Once again, police swooped in to hunt for evidence. That afternoon, another note was found, left on the branch of a fallen tree. It was read immediately, unlike after the Ashland shooting when investigators delayed in reading the note. The second note again repeated the demand for money and the threat to harm children, but this time it said, "Your incompetence has cost you another life."

Hundreds of local police officers and Maryland state troopers—pistols drawn, rifles at the ready—sealed off highway exits and side streets all over the Washington area. The American Legion Bridge between Maryland and Virginia, one of the region's most critical commuter links, was shut down. Thousands of commuters, stranded for hours and frustrated by the traffic snarls, wondered how the sniper had managed to slip through yet another time.

The pressure on law enforcement was intense. Had the failed bust yesterday and the failure to meet the sniper's deadline led to another shooting? Was this the sniper's way of responding to police?

The FBI profilers and negotiators working with the sniper task force advised its leaders not to rush out with a briefing right away. No one wanted to pump up the sniper by giving him that kind of immediate reaction. The profilers and negotiators also told leaders to be careful about showing too much emotion. Montgomery County Executive Doug Duncan, a father of five, was sick with worry. Johnson had been a longtime county employee. One of Duncan's main jobs through the sniper crisis was to try to keep the community—his constituents—on an even keel. He had spent most of his days at police headquarters and going to the funerals of most all the victims. He had been appearing before the cameras to tell people to live normally—go to work, school, shopping, out to dinner. And now, a man doing his job, a county employee, was dead. "You are wondering," said Duncan, a popular politician, Montgomery's top elected official for most of the past decade, "will people die because I've told them to go about their lives?"

The question hung like a pall over the rest of the day.

Chief Moose's noon press conference that Tuesday was a disaster. "We are doing everything in our power to protect people, to get the evidence that we need to get this person or these people off the street," the chief said, adding somberly: "We have not been able to assure anyone of their safety."

There was more than the usual current of tension in the throng of reporters at the briefing. Not only had there been another shooting, but the morning's newspapers had sketchy stories about a note left behind at the Ponderosa Saturday night. Some press accounts had implied that the sniper had threatened children, pointing to that as the reason Richmond school authorities had closed the schools. Reporters pressed Moose about that. He was vague. The sniper, he said, had targeted all kinds of people. Everyone in the region, he said, should be careful. "This person or people involved in this have shown ability and a willingness to kill people of all ages, all races, all genders, at different times of day, different days of the week and different professions."

Police had shared the threat to children with school and other elected officials, but only in the most general terms, and they emphasized that the information, even as vague as it was, was not to be disseminated to the general public. To Moose, Gary Bald, Mike Bouchard and others directing the task force, the threat in the sniper's note was chilling, but not new. No one, including children, was safe. And certainly no one wanted to talk about kids in front of the TV cameras.

But reporters persisted: Would authorities warn the public if the sniper had specifically targeted children? Why hadn't officials in Montgomery County canceled school as they had in the Richmond area for a second day in a row? "Anything we have with regards to the safety of community members," Moose responded calmly but sternly, "we do not feel like this is the forum to have those discussions."

After the press conference, Moose and a few top officials huddled.

They knew it had been a flop. "This did not work," said Duncan, the forty-six-year-old county executive. "We didn't get the message out."

Inside the police command center, there was more debate. The sniper *had* threatened children in his note left in Ashland, but the law enforcement experts didn't want to put that out. The police were worried it might jeopardize the investigation. They didn't want to offend the sniper, who had said not to release the note's contents to the press. Nor did they want to somehow empower him. Nor, it went without saying, did anyone want to invite mass public panic.

But worried parents were trying to decide whether to send their children to school. Montgomery Schools Superintendent Jerry Weast said his office was flooded with calls. Duncan pressed the FBI's Gary Bald: "We need to give the exact language of the note." Sharing that language, Duncan believed, would help calm the public. The public, he believed, would see that the threat was fairly general, and that would defuse tensions.

Meetings were held with the FBI profilers and negotiators to talk about exactly what to share from the sniper's note and how to say it publicly—much the way they had cleared past communications.

There were strong arguments on both sides; powerful, deeply felt emotions in every corner of the room. Bald, Moose and the other police officials, however, felt that the law enforcement prerogatives must take precedence over the political, however legitimate they might be. People would simply have to understand.

"There was no script," Bald said, "for anything."

Billy Sorukas was deep into the sorry life of John Muhammad.

The timeline of the former Gulf War veteran's travels and travails was far from complete, but Sorukas was making rapid progress. At one point he called the command center in Montgomery County with a request. Could someone quickly run Muhammad's name through the FBI's tip line database? Almost immediately, the computer spit out the Rapid Start lead sheet detailing the call on October 17 from Robert Holmes, Muhammad's old army buddy in Tacoma, Washington.

One of Holmes's comments jumped out at Sorukas right away. Muhammad's former wife, Mildred, was supposed to be living in a Washington suburb. Sorukas was more convinced than ever that Muhammad and his young sidekick were the guys.

FBI agents also were poring over the tip from

Holmes. That day, hours after Conrad Johnson was shot on the steps of his bus, several agents conducted an in-depth interview with Holmes at their offices in Tacoma. There, Holmes elaborated on the information he had called in to the tip line. He described what he knew of Muhammad's bitter divorce and said that Mildred Muhammad had accused her former husband of threatening her life. Muhammad had vanished with the couple's three kids for more than a year, Holmes said. Muhammad somehow had learned, Holmes said, that Mildred and the kids were living in the Washington, D.C., region. It was just a matter of time, Muhammad had told Holmes, before he could pinpoint exactly where she was. Holmes told the agents that Muhammad said he was not trying to find Mildred to hurt her. He also told them that he had seen a personality change in Muhammad since he first met him. For instance, Muhammad had made anti-American comments shortly after the September 11 terrorist attacks, he told the agents. Holmes speculated that Muhammad might have had a breakdown of some kind.

The agents took voluminous notes.

Muhammad frequented YMCAs, Holmes said, and used an alias of Wayne Weeks or Wayne Weekley. On his more recent visits to Holmes's house in Tacoma, he said, Muhammad had had a young companion traveling with him—a youth Muhammad referred to as "the sniper." Holmes described the different guns Muhammad had with him on visits earlier in the year, an AR-15 and another rifle. He told them of Muhammad's attempts to build a silencer and his chilling comment, "Can you imagine the damage you could do if you could shoot with a silencer?"

Holmes told the agents that he originally contacted the FBI because he had heard through media reports that an M-16 might be involved in the sniper shootings and because there might be two people involved. But if he were really the sniper, Holmes told the agents, he didn't think Muhammad would be leaving messages for law enforcement. Still, Holmes called it "just a gut feeling that he might be the sniper."

In the bedlam of the Joint Operations Center next door to Chief Moose's police headquarters, the names of John Muhammad and Lee Malvo were placed on the big list of possible suspects.

Around 4:30 P.M., a tired-looking Moose strode to the podium and released the exact language of what the sniper had said about children to show parents that there was no specific threat targeting schools. The police chief delivered a long, carefully crafted statement. After much debate, the decision had been made to share the postscript from the letter the sniper had left behind at the Ponderosa in Ashland.

First, Moose addressed the sniper, his fourth message since Sunday.

"We have received a communication," he said. "We will be responding soon.

"Secondly, there continues to be a great deal of speculation as to a reference, a threat in the message previously received. As stated earlier, everyone knows that all of our citizens are and have been at risk. The person or people have demonstrated a willingness and ability to shoot people of all ages, all races, all genders, and they've struck at different times of the day, different days, at different locations.

"We recognize the concerns of the community and therefore are going to provide the exact language in the message that pertains to the threat. It is in the form of a postscript: 'Your children are not safe anywhere at any time.'

"We feel it's important to provide this information to the public. We are not providing the remaining content of the message. It does not communicate to the public. However, to share that at this point would be detrimental to an investigation. And it will not be released.

"Please understand that this exact language has previously been shared with the leadership, the law enforcement community leadership, people who needed to make decisions. As a result of numerous inquiries and reporting of incorrect versions, different versions, we felt it was important to come out and give the exact version."

The unnerving line that "Your children are not safe anywhere at any time," left a vast region reeling. Parents were wondering where their children were safe. Should they send them to school the next morning? What about the rest of the week? Should they stay home?

What had changed? Why had Moose, the FBI's Gary Bald and the ATF's Mike Bouchard agreed to release that line? Part of it was because they felt like the news stories floating around that day raised more questions than they answered. The officials wanted to make sure the story was straight about what the threat to children really was.

The night before, elected leaders had all agreed not to close schools. At 9 P.M. on Monday, October 21, Montgomery County Executive Doug Duncan had met with top elected leaders from the Washington region—numerous counties from Maryland and Virginia, as well as the District of Columbia—around the big conference table in his office in Rockville. Chief Moose, Bald and Bouchard were there too. It had been a sensitive meeting. Those overseeing the sniper investigation had wanted to share the note's threat to children with these top elected officials. Even though law enforcement officials' instinct is to hold such information close to the vest, they knew this was so important that they had to keep the elected politicians informed. That night, the politicos debated how they should react. "The consensus was to keep kids in school," Duncan told reporters. "The feeling was, children and everyone in this community has been under threat since the shooting started, and particularly since the shooting of the student at Bowie [Iran Brown]." Besides, some people wondered, even if schools were closed, how long would they stay that way? A day? Two days? A week? Until the sniper was caught?

So then, on Tuesday after the noon press conference had gone so badly, Duncan had argued a persuasive case to Moose, Bald and Bouchard to make that line from the note public. Bald looked at Duncan and said that they would agree to release that line publicly, but only that line, "If you are saying this will help."

In such an unprecedented investigation, nothing was written in stone. Yielding to community concerns, the three had assented: They would share with the public the postscript of the note left at the Ponderosa.

It may have looked like capitulation, but nearly

everyone involved said the decision to reverse course on disclosing the contents of the note's postscript was a testament to the candor and openness of the investigators in dealing with the many different constituencies affected by the sniper attacks. There was also abundant evidence that despite the increasing anger of commuters, teachers, parents and business owners over the continued failure to apprehend the sniper, the multifaceted, cobbled-together task force that had been assembled on the fly three weeks earlier was working and working well, despite what many would have given as dauntingly long odds.

At the noon press conference, reporters pressed Bald, demanding to know when the vaunted FBI would take over the sniper investigation. "The circumstances have not changed," Bald told the reporters calmly. "This continues to be a joint investigation by a large number of state, local and federal law enforcement agencies." Putting the FBI in charge of the case, Bald concluded, "would make absolutely no difference in the manner in which the investigation is being conducted," adding that "the cooperation that we have is unprecedented in this case." County Executive Duncan affirmed that the federals, as far as he could see, had been treating their local counterparts as "equal partners." But Duncan also told Chief Moose, who reported to Duncan, that if the case dragged on another week, things were going to get much uglier. The drumbeat for the FBI would only get stronger. The national press would beat them up. And during that last week of the sniper investigation, Duncan met with community leaders to rally support for Moose and the embattled task force.

*   *   *

Shortly after 7 P.M., Moose returned to the cameras.

He had a message for the snipers, his fifth since Sunday evening. "In the past several days, you have attempted to communicate with us. We have researched the options you stated and found that it is not possible electronically to comply in the manner that you requested.

"However, we remain open and ready to talk to you about the options you have mentioned. It is important that we do this without anyone else getting hurt. Call us at the same number you used before to obtain the 800 number that you have requested. If you would feel more comfortable, a private post office box or another secure method can be provided."

For a minute, Moose lowered his head and narrowed his eyes slightly.

"You indicated that this is about more than violence. We are waiting to hear from you."

The press conference ended moments later. Reporters scrambled to file their stories against the late-evening deadlines.

Billy Sorukas was racking his brain.

Somewhere in the bowels of some government agency someplace there simply had to be a photograph of John Muhammad.

But where? Thinking about the thousands of records he had pored over during the past few days, Sorukas suddenly remembered. Muhammad had once applied for and been granted a driver's license in California. Sorukas dialed a friend, Ralph Garofalo. The two had worked together years before in the marshals' office in San Diego, Sorukas's first posting.

"I need a big favor," Sorukas told Garofalo quickly. "I need you to go into the office. Here is the driver's license number. I need it tonight."

A few hours later, sometime after 1 A.M., Garofalo called back. He had the photo. Could he send it via e-mail?

Sorukas was spent. "Yeah, send the e-mail," he said.

"Who is this guy?" Garofalo asked.

He'd been up for days, but suddenly Sorukas felt himself getting a second wind.

"I think," he told Garofalo, "you have just gotten the first look at one of the snipers."

21

"Duck in a Noose"

Wednesday, October 23, seemed endless.

Not long after he got his first glimpse of the photograph of John Muhammad e-mailed from San Diego, Billy Sorukas picked up the phone again and got someone out of bed in West Virginia. There were still hours to go before dawn, but there was no time to waste. This was urgent.

The FBI's Criminal Justice Information Services Division, the Bureau's central repository of files on wanted and convicted criminals of every description, is located in Clarksburg, West Virginia. Sorukas needed someone there—someone who knew the system inside and out—to do what is known as an offline search. He didn't want just a search of FBI records on John Muhammad and Lee Malvo. He faxed a letter seeking a more global search—names, dates of birth, circumstances of an arrest or a traffic stop, the works—to see what records on the two men there might be from other police agencies that might have had contact with them.

At around 6 A.M., Sorukas's fax machine began spitting out a seemingly endless stream of documents. One was dated 10-8-2002, 3:01 A.M. It was from the Baltimore City Police Department. It was impossible to tell from the document whether Baltimore's John Muhammad was the same as the John Muhammad under investigation. The record in front of Sorukas showed which computer terminal had recorded the information: 01H3. But he needed to know more—and quickly. "Someone needs to get up to Baltimore right away," Sorukas told a colleague, "and find out what this inquiry was."

Brian Sheppard, a deputy from the Baltimore marshals' office, got the ticket. Soon, Sheppard and Baltimore police officer Deborah Kirk were plowing through hours of tape recordings trying to find the radio traffic of the officer who had called in the inquiry on a John Muhammad. The first tape they listened to didn't have it. The police officer and the deputy marshal spooled up another one.

Across the region, a faint sun began slipping through the fog, but it would be a morning fraught with gloom and anxiety. The morning news shows and the newspapers' front pages were dominated by the accounts of the sniper's note threatening to attack children. Some kids were kept home from school, but many other students were taken by their parents. Many parents wanted to drop them off at the door rather than putting them on a bus. Police officers in patrol cars staked out schools and escorted buses. Parents used their bodies as shields to protect their children as they ran into buildings.

The schools remained in what the educators called Code Blue, meaning kids still had to stay inside, as they had pretty much been doing since early October. The teachers and students locked inside were stressed. Bus drivers and school crossing guards—the folks who stand exposed on corners with bright vests—didn't call in sick. At one point, a call had gone out for adult volunteers in Montgomery County to take the place of children who served as safety patrols; some twelve hundred people jammed the phone lines offering to fill in for the kids.

New kinds of conversations between parents and children were taking place across the region. It wasn't unusual for a child to wake up and ask: "Any more shootings?" "Any arrests?" "Code Blue again today?" And since Chief Moose's press conference the day before when he revealed the sniper's chilling threat, some kids asked a question that parents found even harder to answer. "What kind of person would want to hurt children?"

There was so much to think about. Election Day was less than a week away. Maryland Governor Parris Glendening was thinking about calling out the National Guard. Halloween was just around the corner, too, but many communities were canceling parades and trying to patch together indoor alternatives to outdoor trick-or-treating.

The sniper was affecting business, too—badly. Starbucks yanked its outdoor tables and chairs. Restaurant sales were down across the region; people were too afraid to go out to dinner. Some just had no appetite. Tourist groups with reservations to Washington events stayed home. Grocery delivery service, on the other hand, was off the charts. Pizza deliveries spiked.

But the biggest effect of all the fear was a constant weariness. The sniper had changed the way people lived. Husbands and wives said good-bye to each other a new way: "Don't get gas today. Love you." Grown men ducked behind shopping carts as a shield to run from the store to the car. Women calculated in advance how fast they could make it to the doctor's or dentist's office with a small child in their arms. Everyone was zigzag walking.

At a noon press conference, Chief Moose confirmed what everyone already knew—the shooting of Conrad Johnson, the genial bus driver who let schoolkids warm their hands in his bus and always had a kind word for his elderly regulars, was the sniper's latest victim.

The chief, once again, appealed for witnesses. Anyone who had seen anything, please, give us a call. Come talk to us. Several of the shootings had occurred in neighborhoods populated by immigrants, Moose noted. He encouraged them not to be afraid of the police. The cops weren't interested in their immigration status. But no matter who they were, Moose said, there would also be no free passes. "We hope that somehow in their heart that they do the right thing, and we will put our energy to help them," he said. "But nobody gets a guarantee on anything. Life doesn't work that way."

Things still weren't working the way everyone hoped in the complicated investigative machinery that had been set up to catch the snipers. Callers to the various tip lines continued to complain about endless busy signals. The lines were staffed around the clock by FBI employees, trainees, and representatives from other agencies. But the volume of the calls was such that even this army of extra recruits couldn't keep up. And after each new shooting, unsurprisingly, the number of calls jumped. "It's not unexpected," Gary Bald told reporters patiently, "that from time to time the number of calls coming in will overtax the system."

Around 3 P.M., John McCain, the former Vietnam prisoner of war, current senator from Arizona, and scourge of his fellow Republicans, added his voice to those of the growing number of critics of the sniper investigation. "All due respect to Chief Moose and all of the other hardworking, dedicated, wonderful people that are working twenty-four hours a day," McCain said on a CNN interview show. "[But] I just think we need an individual in charge, the federal government in charge."

The police were walking a fine line. They were taking pains not to offend the shooter, and they felt that releasing some information that might be helpful to the public would offend him. At the press conference, reporters asked Moose if he would consider alerting the public during times that seemed more vulnerable—such as if a deadline set by the sniper had passed. Moose was clear: "At the foundation of our process, and it is a very emotional process, thoughtful process, but at the bottom line, the three of us, it is always public safety's first and the investigation is second," he said. "That has always been the case, and that will be the case."

Moose's tone when he spoke to the sniper had been so deferential that a television reporter asked him why he had spoken somewhat apologetically, courteously, even respectfully to the sniper from the podium. "Well, sir, my parents, they prefer it if I'm a gentleman at all times," Moose replied. "And so, hopefully, I've been courteous and respectful to you, and no one's asked why. It just seems to be the right thing to do."

"But the sniper's a killer, Chief," the reporter continued.

"Well, sir, I've answered your question," Moose replied.

To Mike Bouchard and Gary Bald, Chief Moose was the face the investigators needed to present not just to the world but, most important, to the snipers. He was decent, steadfast, a man whose very being seemed to convey a sense of trustworthiness. Which made the growing number of calls for a federal takeover of the investigation all the more awkward. The din had grown so loud that even the White House felt compelled to address the issue. In his daily news conference, Press Secretary Ari Fleischer took great pains to detail the resources the federal government had already brought to bear on the sniper investigation. The numbers were impressive: four hundred fifty-four ATF agents; fifty-nine ATF inspectors; nine canine handlers; one hundred one support staff to do laboratory, computer and intelligence work. The U.S. Secret Service provided fifty special agents to the sniper task force. The FBI had six hundred people working on the case, most of them highly trained special agents. The Drug Enforcement Administration and the U.S. Marshals Service also had thrown investigators into the breach. The U.S. Customs Service had provided two A-Star light-lift helicopters with twenty-person flight teams, as well as offered on-demand use of a Black Hawk helicopter. The Pentagon had put surveillance planes at the investigation's disposal. The Department of Education had ponied up generous sums for schools in Maryland and Virginia to use for anything from student and teacher counseling to additional security.

The message was clear. If the task force investigators hadn't caught the snipers yet, it wasn't for lack of resources. This was an investigation with a degree of difficulty that few in law enforcement had ever experienced before. It was not a case, obviously, that would be broken easily or quickly.

On Wednesday afternoon, Billy Sorukas got a call from the command center in Rockville. Investigators needed about three hundred or four hundred photos of John Muhammad. Pronto.

It wasn't exactly in his job description, but Sorukas started cranking out photos like a MotoPhoto clerk. It made sense, though. The more pictures they could put out there of Muhammad, the more likely someone would spot him and place a call to police.

Throughout the day, investigators armed with photos called on homeless shelters and YMCAs, passing around photos of Muhammad and Malvo. Detectives canvassed motels. If Muhammad and Malvo were in the area, eventually someone was bound to see them.

Finally, the break they had been waiting for.

Brian Sheppard and Deborah Kirk were wiped out from listening to the hours and hours of police tapes, but finally they had found what they were looking for. Officer James Snyder, working the midnight shift on October 8, had radioed in for a check on a 1990 Chevrolet Caprice that had been parked near a Subway. A man had been sleeping inside. A check of the

New Jersey tag numbers had revealed nothing problematic. Ditto the man's driver's license. As far as the computers knew, John Muhammad was not an individual the police had any cause to take a special interest in.

Billy Sorukas flew into action. At times like these, seasoned investigators force themselves to take a breath, remind themselves to assume as little as possible. There was no saying what the odds were that the man in the Caprice questioned by Snyder was the same man who had been keeping company with Lee Malvo, whose print had been found on the gun catalog from Montgomery, Alabama. The driver's license Snyder saw said John Muhammad. But that's not an entirely uncommon name. Were the two one and the same? Sorukas's nose twitched. He thought maybe he should get a photograph of John Muhammad sent to Snyder—immediately. If the patrol officer made the photograph as the same guy he had rousted for sleeping in the Caprice, they had a match. But before he could order up the photo, Sheppard mentioned that the driver's license Snyder had run had been issued in Washington State. That's where John Muhammad had hooked up with Lee Malvo. And that's when Sorukas knew—call it a cop's intuition—this was their guy.

At the Joint Operations Center in Rockville, Mike Moran of the U.S. Marshals waved over Capt. Barney Forsythe from the Montgomery County Police Department and showed him the make, model and tag number of the car.

Forsythe's eyes widened. "Is that the car?"

Moran grabbed Dan Kumor. Bingo! The veteran ATF agent grabbed a microphone. The room was so noisy there was no other way to communicate. Using the room's PA system, Kumor announced: "We have a license plate and the car they're driving."

Everyone was pumped. But then, the place went right back to work.

Some investigators were worried, though.

Should they release the car's description to the public right away? Wait? What if the snipers heard news accounts describing the car? They could simply ditch it and go underground. What if these weren't really the snipers? That was still a possibility, a real one.

On the other side of the nation, a small army of federal investigators fanned out across Washington State. FBI agents descended on Fort Lewis, the army post south of Tacoma. Others poured into Bellingham. In Fort Lewis, the agents politely requested records, everything the army had on a former soldier named John Williams. In Bellingham, agents pursued inquiries about two people—a teenage boy who had been a student briefly at Bellingham High and an older man with whom the boy spent a lot of time.

At around 1:30 P.M., FBI and ATF agents used yellow crime-scene tape to make a grid in Robert Holmes's backyard in Tacoma, using metal detectors to search for spent shell casings and bullet fragments. They tore up the backyard and used a chain saw to dig out a tree stump containing a bullet fragment. They carted the mess away in a rented U-Haul. Chris Waters, a Fort Lewis soldier who lived across the street from the Holmes house, told reporters that he had heard "high-powered rifle fire" at night for about four weeks in January 2002.

The backyard search was broadcast live on national television, a move that made some investigators cringe. If Muhammad and Malvo spotted it, they would know investigators were on to them. It was a definite risk. But there was nothing that could be done. The search had to be done.

Late Wednesday, Special Agent Craig Howe, assigned to the ATF's office in Seattle, asked federal magistrate Monica J. Benton to issue an arrest warrant for John Allen Muhammad. The charge: possession of a firearm by a person subject to a restraining order. Howe's petition said that the Pierce County Superior Court in Tacoma had decided, on March 17, 2000, that Muhammad had committed domestic violence, forbidding him from "causing physical harm . . . molesting, harassing, threatening or stalking" Mildred Muhammad and their three children. ATF agent Howe also said he had reviewed state Firearm Transfer Form No. Z-10, which showed that on May 23, 2000, Muhammad had transferred a Bushmaster rifle, .223-caliber, model A-35, XM15-E2S, serial number L166036. Welcher's Gun Shop in Tacoma said that John Muhammad had bought the gun for eight hundred dollars on December 28, 1999—before the restraining order went into effect, Afterward, in May, Muhammad sold the weapon back to the store for five hundred dollars.

At 9:09 P.M., a BOLO message went out to law enforcement agencies throughout the country. The decision was made to mention Lee Malvo, saying that he might be in the company of John Muhammad. The alert to police also included a description of the blue 1990 Chevrolet Caprice with the New Jersey license NDA-21Z.

The debate within the task force about releasing the information had finally been resolved. The FBI wanted to make the names and photos public. The ATF was a little more reluctant. What if these men weren't the snipers? No one wanted another Richard Jewell situation. No one wanted to ruin reputations or, worse, jeopardize their safety if they weren't the snipers. "Everyone was nervous—what if it was the wrong person," Doug Duncan said later. But Gary Bald said, "I knew the pictures had to be out there." He said he didn't want to be in the position of withholding such information in case another shooting occurred. "I wanted to make sure that didn't happen."

At 10:02 P.M., CNN reported that police were seeking a 1990 Caprice with New Jersey plates. CNN reporter Kelli Arena told viewers, "We have been cautioned not to refer to these individuals as suspects." Moments later, MSNBC's Pete Williams said, "We have been asked not to pass these specific names on."

Then, at 10:52 P.M., Fox's Rita Cosby reported that police were looking for John Allen Williams or John Muhammad and Lee Malvo. Cosby gave the New Jersey tag number as NDA-21Z.

The news was out.

Chief Moose stepped in front of the TV cameras at 11:50 P.M.

He did not mention that authorities were viewing Muhammad as a suspect in the sniper shootings. The police, the chief said, were merely looking to speak with him, although Muhammad was wanted in connection with other matters. Moose elaborated, somewhat. Muhammad, the chief said, was "armed and extremely dangerous." He was being sought for "alleged violation of federal firearms laws." But the chief also added "a strong word of caution: Do not assume from this allegation that John Allen Muhammad . . . is involved in any of the shootings we are investigating." He said the warrant for Muhammad's arrest "was not related to the recent shootings under investigation" by the task force but added that Muhammad "may have information material to our investigation."

Moose issued a photograph of a clean-shaven man with a cropped haircut. He described Muhammad as six foot one and one hundred eighty pounds and said he might be accompanied by a juvenile.

At the same time, Moose spoke directly to the killer, who had told police he wanted to be described as caught "like a duck in a noose."

Moose's direct, high-stakes message to the sniper was his sixth message since Sunday and seemed to imply that the effort to communicate had been rocky and unsuccessful. "We understand that you communicated with us by calling several different locations. Our inability to talk has been a concern to us, as it has been for you.

"You have indicated that you want us to do and say certain things. You've asked us to say, quote, We have caught the sniper like a duck in a noose, end quote. We understand that hearing us say this is important to you.

"However, we want you to know how difficult it has been to understand what you want because you have chosen to use only notes, indirect messages and calls to other jurisdictions. The solution remains to call us and get a private toll-free number established just for you.

"We still ask you to call or write us at P.O. Box 7875, Gaithersburg, Md., 20898-7875.

"If you are reluctant to contact us, be assured that we remain ready to talk, directly with you. Our word is our bond.

"If we can establish communications with you, we can offer other means of addressing what you have asked us for. Let's talk directly. We have an answer for you about your option. We are waiting for you to contact us."

The duck in a noose reference appeared to come from a folk tale in which an arrogant rabbit tries to catch a duck in a noose. The duck seems to have been caught but then flies off, dragging the rabbit with him. Then, the rabbit falls into a tree stump, where he is trapped.

Mike Bouchard got home around 1 A.M. and fell straight into a dreamless sleep. Gary Bald headed back to his hotel but discovered that his room had been given away. The hotel couldn't find him another one, so the FBI veteran drove north, looking for a place to lay his head. He had just checked into a Holiday Inn when his cell phone rang.

The Caprice had been found.

Bald dropped his suitcase and climbed back into his car.

22

Captured

It was nearly 1 A.M. on Thursday, October 24, and Whitney Donahue was on his way home after working the night shift. A supermarket refrigeration specialist from Greencastle, Pennsylvania, Donahue was a man meticulous about detail. Listening to a talk show on his car radio, he had heard an announcer give a description of the car police were searching for in connection with all the sniper shootings. The announcer gave the car's make and description, along with the license number. As he later explained on ABC's *Good Morning America*, Donahue scribbled the information down on his time sheet. A few minutes later, he pulled into a rest stop at mile marker forty-two on Interstate 70. He was eleven miles west of Frederick, Maryland, and still had a good way to go before he made it home.

There were just two cars parked in the automobile-parking area of the rest stop. One, Donahue realized immediately, was the vehicle described by the radio news announcer. Donahue checked his time sheet. Sure enough, it was a Chevrolet Caprice with New Jersey plates. It had backed into a parking spot.

Donahue pulled his van in directly across from the Caprice and tried to call police twice on his cell phone. The connection was bad and he couldn't get through. He decided to visit the men's room, then moved his van and tried to call again. This time, at 12:47 A.M. he got patched through to the Frederick County Sheriff's Office. Donahue told the dispatcher about the Caprice and read off the New Jersey plate number.

"Hold on," the dispatcher said.

The dispatcher asked Donahue a question. Could he keep an eye on the Caprice for a while, until some police officers got there? Donahue said he would try. The dispatcher kept the phone line open. Donahue eyed the area where the Caprice was from his seat in the van. He was a nervous wreck.

David Reichenbaugh left the Joint Operations Center late, as usual.

The top intelligence officer for the Maryland State Police, Reichenbaugh had had a migraine for nearly three weeks straight. He'd been putting in eighteen-hour days but didn't complain. Everyone else was, too. Tired as he was, Reichenbaugh grabbed a stack of flyers the task force had just had printed up with the photos of Muhammad and Malvo. Before he headed home to Frederick, he planned to stop by the State Police barracks near his home and spread the flyers around.

Reichenbaugh was on Interstate 270 when he got

a call from the duty sergeant: "We believe we have a sighting of the vehicle."

"Send every trooper you've got," Reichenbaugh commanded.

Reichenbaugh tensed. The Interstate was his turf. The terrain around it was rolling and wooded. Over the radio in his cruiser, he directed troopers from the Frederick barracks to surround the rest stop at mile marker forty-two. "No matter what you have to do," Reichenbaugh ordered, "these people do not leave this rest area tonight. Do not let them out of the rest area."

Reichenbaugh was worried. The snipers had a high-powered rifle that could shred a cop's bullet-proof vest. His guys had handguns.

Within minutes, Reichenbaugh's troopers had shut down I-70 in both directions. The rest stop was dark, but there were a number of eighteen-wheelers in the truck-parking area. Working quickly, Reichenbaugh woke up several truckers and asked them to block the exit. "Do you want to be a good American?" he asked one trucker.

The trucker said he did.

"We believe the sniper is in the rest stop," Reichenbaugh said. "Use your truck to block as much of this road as possible. Stay in your cab."

Minutes later, the rest stop was sealed off. Still, Reichenbaugh was worried. What if whoever was in the Caprice tried to make a run for it across I-70? He radioed for some canine units. They quickly assumed positions on the Interstate's grassy median.

"If anyone comes running out of the woods, let the dogs eat them," Reichenbaugh barked. "Anyone on foot is a bad guy."

The troopers didn't want to get too close to the Caprice just yet, lest they make a commotion. At this point, Larry Blank, the midnight-shift rest-stop attendant, was sitting inside Whitney Donahue's van, helping to keep tabs on the car. They would stay on the phone with police for nearly three hours. Reichenbaugh asked custodian Blank if he had seen the men in the car before he got into Donahue's van. Blank said he hadn't seen anyone in the car.

Reichenbaugh was worried. Were the snipers loose?

The SWAT team showed up next.

It was a multiagency show. FBI, ATF, Montgomery County police, the state cops—each had officers trained to perform the dangerous and demanding jobs that usually fell to the Special Weapons and Tactics teams.

SWAT would handle the takedown of the Caprice.

The team arrived in choppers and patrol cars, lights out. Gary Bald had ditched his coat and tie, but was very much in charge. At the rest stop, he had the FBI's hostage rescue team describe their plan. In detail.

At 3:19 A.M., two dozen flak-jacketed cops and federal agents tossed a flash-bang grenade into the Caprice. Flash-bangs are basically harmless, but they can scare the hell out of someone—they emit a blindingly bright flash and come accompanied by a loud bang. With much screaming, members of the SWAT team smashed one of the Caprice's filthy windows.

Seconds later, John Muhammad and Lee Malvo were yanked out of the disgusting sedan, littered with old clothes and greasy fast-food wrappers. The two men stared blankly at the heavily armed police officers in front of them. In grimy jeans and sweatshirts, Muhammad and Malvo smelled like they hadn't showered in days.

"Man, if you would have gotten that ten million," one of the arresting officers said, just before they were placed in handcuffs and led away, "I hope you would have at least bought a bar of soap."

There was still much to be done.

After Muhammad and Malvo were taken away, FBI Special Agent Michael McCoy and ATF Special Agent Scott Riordan filed a hasty application in federal court to search the Caprice. The sniper task force had made what looked like two good arrests. Now the members of the team and the men in charge of it had to make sure they stuck. U.S. Magistrate Judge Jillyn Schulze signed the warrant presented by the agents, but no one was going to "just toss the car," as Gary Bald put it. "It's a methodical search."

In the early morning light, the investigating officers made a chilling discovery. The trunk of the battered Caprice had been converted into a sniper's nest. The backseat was rigged so it could be flipped down, allowing someone to lie in the trunk. A hole had been cut in the trunk above the keyhole to accommodate a gun's scope and barrel. When the hole wasn't in use, Muhammad and Malvo stuck a blue sock into it.

The rifle was a Bushmaster XM15-E2S .223-caliber rifle, serial number L284320. The officer conducting the search of the Caprice discovered it behind the car's backseat. When the officers found it, the other cops and federal agents watching the proceedings cheered as though their favorite team had just scored a touchdown in overtime. The gun was whisked off to the FBI lab to be analyzed for DNA evidence. Next it would go to the ATF crime lab in Rockville. There, firearms examiner Walt Dandridge—the same expert who had analyzed all the fragments from the shootings—would test-fire the weapon into a tank of water and retrieve the projectile, now cleanly tattooed with the gun's unique signature markings.

Piece by careful piece, the evidence was starting to pile up.

Dandridge spent six hours doing what is known as a "side-by-side comparison." It's a lot like matching two puzzle pieces. He compared the fragments recovered as evidence with the newly fired slug, trying to match what are called "lands and grooves" on both with each other. Dandridge could have compared only one fragment from one of the shootings. That would have been enough to declare the Bushmaster the crime gun. But the ATF's Bouchard wanted to be able to definitively offer each of the families some kind of closure. "We felt we owed it to each of the victims' families to say this gun was the one that killed your loved one," he said.

The full search of the Caprice eventually would yield a cache of shooting gear. Besides the gun, police found a single brown cotton glove. It was sticking out of the hole in the trunk, the apparent mate to another single brown cotton glove that had been found two days before at the scene of Conrad Johnson's shooting. There were quite a few papers with handwritten notes on them. On the ground outside the car, officers found two shooting mittens. They had been taken from John Muhammad when he was arrested. They found a green military Alice pack outside the car containing a global positioning system. On the ground outside the car, officers also found a paper towel similar to the kind used at gas stations—and a single .223 round was underneath it. On the hood, they found a wallet containing driver's licenses in different names but all bearing Muhammad's photo, including Washington State driver's license MUHJA402RU. Inside the wallet, they also found an AT&T calling card that had been used to make a call at 5:15 P.M., October 3, from a business phone in the 7800 block of Georgia Avenue NW in Washington, D.C.—just a few hours before Pascal Charlot was shot near there.

Other items found were clothing, a NASCAR road atlas, a pair of walkie-talkies, a Sony laptop computer, a pair of sneakers on the floor of the front driver's side, and a jug of water on the front passenger side. There was more stuff: two boxes of Winchester .338 Magnum ammunition, some CDs and a CD case, books, tools in cases, a pair of bolt cutters, a gallon jug of yellow liquid, a section of garden hose and a spare tire.

It was at once pathetic and bizarre, a shooting gallery on wheels.

Muhammad and Malvo were taken to a Montgomery County police building away from headquarters and the media horde. There, they were placed in separate interview rooms. Almost immediately, Malvo tried to escape. He slipped one handcuff off, put a chair on the table and was climbing through a ceiling tile when police officers heard a loud bang. They barged through the door and pulled Malvo off the ceiling. He was covered with drywall dust and looked like a disheveled ghost.

Muhammad, incredibly, had fallen asleep in the police cruiser on the ride from the rest stop. In the interview room, he offered to talk a bit, not much. Malvo, though, responded to detectives with gestures, charades, even tracing out sentences in response to detectives' statements. About the relationship between the two, Malvo indicated they were as close as blood brothers, making a motion as if he were cutting his finger with blood trickling out. At times, Malvo was playful and childlike, but he cried when asked about the last shooting of bus driver Conrad Johnson, leading some investigators to believe that something had gone wrong there. But what that might have been, the cops didn't know.

At least not yet.

News of the predawn capture at the rest stop had everyone talking.

Almost palpably, the fear that had gripped people living in the greater Washington area seemed to begin to lift. Suddenly, Halloween was back on. School doors were quickly unlocked. Recess resumed. Field trips were resurrected. No more crouching behind gas pumps. No more zigzag walking down the street.

People started making plans for an outdoor weekend, the first in nearly a month.

Later in the day, U.S. Magistrate Judge Beth Gesner ordered John Muhammad held on charges that his possession of a firearm violated the restraining order his ex-wife had obtained against him. He was accompanied by federal public defender James Wyda. Lee Malvo was taken to a hearing closed to the public because he was a juvenile.

Billy Sorukas of the U.S. Marshals took a moment to reflect on the case that had consumed the lives of more than a thousand officers and agents for three full weeks. He noticed the same pattern he had seen in many other cases. Investigators, Sorukas had noticed over the years, often tend to overestimate criminals' abilities. As a result, sometimes police forget about mundane investigative steps. How did the sniper suspects get caught? By sleeping in a suspicious car at a public rest stop.

How smart is that?

In the evening, most of the police chiefs and sheriffs who had had shootings in their jurisdictions were milling around Chief Moose's office, waiting for the ATF's Walt Dandridge to finish his painstaking tests. When word finally came, the room erupted in clapping and cheering. Three minutes later, the leaders of the sniper task force were in front of the podium for the long-awaited evening press conference. A mob of people had shown up—a girls' hockey team, people bearing balloons and cookies. Morton's, the famous steak house, would deliver steak dinners later that night. The flower arrangements and fruit baskets just wouldn't stop coming.

In a steady rain at nearly 8 P.M., Chief Moose, Gary Bald and Mike Bouchard stepped forward. Moose looked exhausted. He took a deep breath and began by asking for a moment of silence for Virginia state trooper Mark Cosslett, who had died Wednesday afternoon in a motorcycle accident on Interstate

95 while on his way to investigate gunshots. Then, Moose said: "We are gathered to hear some information with regards to a sniper situation that has been occurring in the Washington metropolitan area."

Formal as a deacon, right to the end.

The chief introduced Bald. The FBI man recapped the early morning arrest. After Bald and Bouchard, familiar faces by now, Moose took pains to introduce the leadership of the entire team: Don Thompson, the FBI chief in Richmond; Van Harp, the top man in the FBI's Washington field office; Jeff Roehm, special agent of the ATF's Washington field office; Michael Stenger, special agent in charge of the U.S. Secret Service's Washington field office; Charles Ramsey, chief of police in Washington, D.C.; Gerald Wilson, police chief in Prince George's County; Ronald Knight, sheriff in Spotsylvania County; Thomas Manger, police chief in Fairfax County; Charlie Deane, police chief in Prince William County; Lt. Col. Steven Wright, representing Hanover County sheriff Stuart Cook; Ashland Police Chief Frederic Pleasants Jr., unable to make it because of illness; Dave Mitchell, superintendent of the Maryland State Police; Lt. Col. Don Martin, representing Col. W. Gerald Massengill of the Virginia State Police; and U.S. Marshal Johnny Hughes, representing all marshals.

"Certainly this team is larger," Moose said, "but its unprecedented cooperation has made this case possible."

Next, Bouchard delivered the news everyone had wanted to hear: Test results of the Bushmaster rifle found in the car showed it was the weapon that had been used in eleven of the fourteen sniper shootings in which ten people were killed and three wounded.

"We have the weapon," Moose added. "It is off the street."

Quietly, Doug Duncan read a list of the names of the victims and paused for a moment of silence: "James Martin. Sonny Buchanan. Premkumar Walekar. Sarah Ramos. Lori Lewis-Rivera. Pascal Charlot. Dean Meyers. Ken Bridges. Linda Franklin. And Conrad Johnson."

Chief Moose thanked the investigators and citizens who had called in with tips. "We have not given in to the terror," he concluded. "Yes, we've all experienced anxiety. But in the end, resiliency has won out."

Moose then, improbable as it might have seemed even just a few days earlier, thanked the reporters who had made his life such an ordeal those past three weeks. "I would be remiss if I don't acknowledge the cooperation that we received from the media in conveying that many messages that we've needed in order to bring this case to where it is tonight."

Later, Moose reflected that spending time with the victims' families earlier that afternoon reminded him why law enforcement officers take an oath. "We do it for those victims and their families," he said. "So we will never forget. We'll never know their pain, and we only wish we could have stopped this to reduce the number of victims."

As the twenty-three days of terror drew to a close, Moose made it clear that night that the work of the sniper task force was far from over. "We think we put some of the giant pieces of the puzzle together, but there is more," he said. "If you thought somehow that tonight meant that all of the task forces were packing boxes and going home, we're still working. We're going to make sure we give everything our prosecutors need.

" . . . We're going to let a lot of the members of the task force go home, hug their children, hug their spouses and just think about the fact that we continue to live in the greatest nation."

282 28 DAYS OF TERROR

23

"We're Still Working"

Friday, October 25, was overcast, misty and chilly, but no one cared. It could have been raining buckets, and people still would have been standing outside. It was almost hard to believe that the sniper siege was over. It really hit Montgomery County Executive Doug Duncan that morning when he noticed something missing. What *was* it? Finally, it dawned on him: no helicopters whirring overhead. They had become part of the white noise of the suburbs. And now they were gone.

Around the world, the morning's newspaper headlines proclaimed the news: CAUGHT! screamed the New York *Daily News.* THANK GOD, IT'S OVER, declared the *Washington Times.* CAPTURED, said the *Richmond Times-Dispatch. The Independent* in London announced: AT 3 AM, THE POLICE SWOOP AND END AMERICA'S LIVING NIGHTMARE. But drained residents of Washington, D.C., and even the rest of the country were left with an uneasy sense of vulnerability. As in the days after the 9/11 attack on the Pentagon and anxthrax-laced letters, Washington residents once again readjusted their sense of "normal." People felt grateful for mundane acts such as walking down the sidewalk without scanning the horizon. But the sniper siege had shown the entire world just how easily a region of people—in America's capital, no less—could be paralyzed. "Every citizen in our country felt vulnerable," said Hanover County Sheriff V. Stuart Cook, who handled the Ponderosa shooting. "It took away some of our feelings of confidence that we are safe. The nation lost its innocence a year earlier after the nine-eleven terrorist attacks. Now along comes the snipers, which opened the wound even more so."

As Chief Moose had put it at his press conference the night before, investigators had fit together many giant puzzle pieces. But that was just the start. The next morning, the phones at the JOC kept ringing, fax machines were churning, and coffee was stewing in pots far too long. Task No. 1: Building a timeline of John Muhammad and Lee Malvo's activities leading up to the October shootings. Police departments across the country began reviewing their files of mysterious shootings. And prosecutors were jockeying to try the two suspects—with the unseemly, transparent desire to be the first to convict and ultimately execute them.

Back at the JOC, investigators worked hard on retracing the pair's actions, a job that would continue for weeks. Working backward, the investigators began putting together more puzzle pieces to document a bizarre sequence of events that culminated with the sniper shootings on one coast—and that almost certainly began with at least one killing on another, nearly a year earlier. In between, there appear to have been many more shootings, killings, robberies and other crimes.

How had the pair been able to drift from state to state without detection? That was an important question some in law enforcement—and certainly the public—were asking.

But there were other key questions as well: Why had John Allen Muhammad's life spun out of control with such destructive force? Why had Lee Malvo been such a faithful disciple? Investigators sought those answers as they started to interview people who had had contact with the pair. But even weeks later, many investigators still shook their heads and said they really didn't know *why* the rampage had taken place. Some investigators, however, believe that by October, Muhammad and Malvo were inured to killing. What appears to have changed in the Washington, D.C., region, however, was the compressed intensity of the violence—and the white-hot focus of media attention it generated. Suddenly, a middle-aged man and a troubled teenager who hadn't seemed to be able to make anything in life work for them were the stuff of endless TV news coverage.

Investigators would have many entries to their timeline. An early one: February 16, 2002, two days before Malvo's seventeenth birthday. That first killing, it appears, was personal and not at all random.

Keenya Cook had moved into her aunt's house in a hillside Tacoma neighborhood. That Saturday evening, Cook's aunt, Isa Nichols, went to the grocery store. Keenya, just twenty-one, was in the house with her six-month-old daughter. The young woman answered the front door, and someone fired a .45-caliber shot at her face. When Nichols returned around 7:30 P.M., she found Cook collapsed in the doorway, chicken burning on the stove, and the baby upstairs.

For months, police had no leads. When Muhammad's face was broadcast after the sniper arrests, Cook's family made the connection. Police would link the shooting to a gun Muhammad had borrowed from a friend in Tacoma. Unlike later shootings, the slaying seems to have been an act of revenge. Her aunt, Isa Nichols, had kept the books for Muhammad's failed auto repair business. But she had sided with Mildred Muhammad in the custody dispute.

Next on investigators' timeline: March 19. In Bellingham, Malvo had boasted of killing two golfers in Arizona. After the sniper arrests, Arizona investigators reopened the mysterious murder of a sixty-year-old golfer named Jerry Taylor. No mere duffer, Taylor made his own clubs and played nearly every day after work. That Tuesday, the salesman had driven to the city-owned Fred Enke Golf Course in Tucson. He had been practicing alone in the chipping area when he was hit with a single shot to the torso from a long distance by a high-powered rifle. Someone then dragged Taylor's body fifty feet to an isolated area of scrub brush. Other golfers found his body at 2:14 P.M.

After the sniper arrests, FBI and ATF agents and Tucson police scoured the chipping area. They learned that Muhammad and Malvo had been in Tucson then, visiting Muhammad's sister. She lived just blocks from the golf course. Did Muhammad or

Malvo murder Taylor? "We've got a lot of circumstances that point [in that] direction," a law enforcement official said. "But there's nothing conclusive."

Other evidence emerged from that Arizona trip. Police believe Muhammad and Malvo stole the credit card of the Greyhound bus driver who took them out of Tucson on March 25. On April 9, the driver's Visa card was used to buy twelve dollars and one cent in gas at a Tacoma station. The Visa account had been an early clue for investigators: It was the one the snipers had left on the note outside the Ponderosa restaurant demanding ten million dollars.

In April, Muhammad and Malvo were back in Bellingham, crashing with college students in a crowded townhouse. Muhammad had yet another phony story to tell: He claimed he was taking his son on a cross-country journey before college in Jamaica started. "The relationship was like a friendship, like they were buddies," said Jason Hamilton, twenty-four. He assumed his houseguests were homeless because each wore the same sweatshirts and jeans every day. Each toted a duffel bag. Malvo wore a black T-shirt with the words Sniper, from the British Columbia Rifle Association. They had no car. But they were into hygiene, nutrition and a healthy lifestyle. Days, they watched movie videos, and nights, they sacked out on pull-out couches in the living room. "They were great houseguests," said Hamilton. "They were easy to talk to, pretty knowledgeable about a lot of things. They were very personable." Muhammad and Malvo did the dishes, vacuumed and even picked up other people's messes.

* * *

As investigators kept working backward, it became clear that one thing very much on Muhammad's mind during these months was fashioning a silencer. Harjeet Singh met the pair at the Community Food Co-op in Bellingham for tea one day in April. The conversation did not consist of the kind of pleasantries one might expect during an afternoon tea. Muhammad, Singh told police, asked if he knew of any machine shops in British Columbia operated by the East Indian community that could help him make a silencer. Muhammad then showed Singh two pieces of paper with professionally drawn blueprints for a silencer. He said Muhammad also had a book about silencers. Another time, Muhammad showed him a round piece of steel with threads on one end. The chrome-colored pipe was about eight inches long and two inches in diameter. He said Muhammad told him it was a silencer for a rifle.

Muhammad, Singh later told police, had said he wanted to shoot a police officer and then plant a bomb at the funeral so that he could kill more officers.

In May, Muhammad and Malvo also visited with Muhammad's former army buddy Robert Holmes at his Tacoma duplex. Muhammad called Malvo "the sniper" and told his old friend they had met in the Caribbean. Holmes nicknamed the kid "Little High Ginseng." Muhammad told Holmes his associate was a sniper. The teen carried his clothes around in a green military-style duffel bag. Muhammad and Malvo carried an AR-15 broken down in a gun case. Holmes later told the FBI that they also had either a 303 or a 30-06 rifle in a black plastic guitar-type case.

During a later visit to Holmes's house, Muhammad had his AR-15 rifle with a scope in an aluminum briefcase. Muhammad and Malvo told Holmes they were taking the AR-15 to the range to "zero it," or calibrate the scope to shoot more accurately.

Another entry to the timeline: In early May, Rabbi Mark Glickman was conducting Saturday morning services at Tacoma's Temple Beth El. When he opened the ark, which contained the sacred Torah, he noticed plaster dust inside. Must be a mouse, he thought. Then, he saw a hole in the ark's rear wall. He eventually traced the holes to the wall across from the ark, then realized they led all the way outside. Police later traced two bullets found at the synagogue to a .44-Magnum borrowed from the same friend who had lent them the .45-caliber semiautomatic used to kill Keenya Cook.

It's unclear exactly when or how Muhammad and Malvo obtained the Bushmaster XM-15. The gun was delivered July 2 to Bull's Eye Shooter Supply near downtown Tacoma. There, it was equipped with several accessories, including grips, a bipod and a laser sight. The whole package was valued at one thousand six hundred dollars. The rifle was displayed behind a sales counter with other weapons. Sometime afterward, it vanished.

After the sniper arrests, investigators traced the gun to Bull's Eye. ATF agents combed through store records, looking for sales documents, but found none.

Investigators learned of a late July trip to Muhammad's hometown of Baton Rouge. On a Saturday afternoon, Janet Scott got a call from her old high school classmate. Muhammad told her a tale about his life. Finally, he said, he had found contentment. He and Mildred, he said, were living happily in the islands. He was starting an export business. He regularly volunteered at his children's school. Mildred's mother, he said, lived with them. God, he told her, had blessed him financially. "I'm not bragging, my sister," he told her. Scott was impressed by how well he was doing.

But Muhammad didn't fool his cousin Edward Holiday, who knew immediately something was wrong. Muhammad looked tired and unkempt. The last time Holiday had seen him in January, Muhammad looked slim and toned, in black pants, a white shirt and shiny black shoes. By summer, however, he looked like a homeless person. "He wasn't the same John to me," said Holiday, who was convinced this would be the last time he would see his cousin.

The pair acted strangely with others in Baton Rouge. They made two trips to Our Daily Bread, a health food store, spending nearly an hour there each time. Malvo wore a long, heavy coat—even though it was sweltering outside. Carrying a backpack, the teenager strolled the aisles, filling a basket, while Muhammad chatted with cashier Sharla Greenwood as if to distract her. He told her he was a "consultant from Canada." When Malvo was done, his basket was empty, and they left without buying a thing. The same thing happened the second time, but they bought a frozen nondairy ice cream substitute. Then, a man working out at the YMCA called the store to report that a man who claimed to be a "consultant from Canada" was selling nutritional supplements at the gym and that one bottle had the price tag of Our

Daily Bread. Store manager Mike Broussard called the police, but there wasn't enough evidence to file charges.

Like so many others, Broussard noticed the unusual dynamic between the two. "The older guy was calling the shots," Broussard said. "I don't think it was physical abuse, but you could tell he was intimidating him. The younger one seemed nervous, sort of shy."

Next on the timeline: By early September, Muhammad and Malvo were in the Washington, D.C., suburbs, drawn to the area, some investigators believe, because Mildred Muhammad was there.

They hung out at the YMCA in Silver Spring, Maryland. Receptionist Sharon Douglas immediately noticed Muhammad, tall, handsome, charming, with a good-looking, polite teenager in tow. When they signed in, using their Washington State membership cards, Sharon Douglas noticed they had the same first name, John. "Oh, is that your son?" she asked him. Muhammad smiled and replied, "Yes." Malvo sometimes was calling himself "John" after Muhammad.

The older man dominated the boy. "When they came in, they were always smiling and friendly," said Douglas. "Mr. Muhammad had more control over the younger one. I never heard him say anything. He always just followed him around." During their regular afternoon workouts, Muhammad swam laps, used the treadmill and lifted free weights. Malvo played basketball or rode the exercise bike.

As they looked backward, investigators would learn that the first shootings leading to the sniper spree may have occurred in September. Most took place when people were locking up businesses. In all, seven people were killed or wounded. Most involved robberies. Some were at closer range than the killings with the Bushmaster. These shootings began in Maryland, but there were others in Georgia, Alabama, and Louisiana. In some cases, witnesses saw a dark sedan leaving the scene.

At the time, no one detected a pattern. Some had occurred outside liquor stores, often high-crime areas. Also, most police departments tend to view crime as a local phenomenon.

Next on the timeline: September 5. Around 10:30 P.M., Paul LaRuffa had locked up Margellina's Pizzeria, in Clinton, Maryland, about a mile from where Mildred Muhammad was living. Sitting in his car, he noticed a shadow to his left, saw a flash and heard a sound "like a cannon." He felt the first bullet go into his arm, then five more .22-caliber shots came through his window. "I was waiting to die," he said later. A friend saw a slight man grab LaRuffa's briefcase with three thousand seven hundred dollars and a black Sony Vaio laptop from the backseat. LaRuffa, fifty-five, didn't die. Bullets punctured his arm, chest, stomach, diaphragm, spleen and back. Police found his laptop in Muhammad's 1990 Chevrolet Caprice after his arrest at the rest stop.

Next stop: Camden, New Jersey. Muhammad and Malvo had come looking for a man they had met in Antigua but found his brother, Nathaniel Osbourne, instead. Muhammad wanted to buy a car, he said, for his son. They found the 1990 Caprice at Sure Shot

Auto Sales in Trenton. It had nearly one hundred forty-seven thousand miles on the odometer.

It caught Muhammad's eye immediately.

Muhammad bought the car for two hundred fifty dollars on September 10. The next day, while the rest of the country was remembering those who had died in the terrorist attacks against the World Trade Center and the Pentagon one year earlier, Muhammad registered the Caprice and was issued the New Jersey tags. He listed Nathaniel Osbourne as a co-owner. (Authorities tracked down Osbourne but didn't charge him, saying he hadn't committed any wrongdoing.)

Back to Maryland: September 14. Around 10:15 P.M., Arnie Zelkovitz was showing his employee, Rupinder Oberoi, twenty-two, how to lock up his store, Hillandale Beer and Wine in Silver Spring, close to the Capital Beltway. Zelkovitz heard a sound like something heavy falling on a tin roof.

"I'm hurt, I'm hurt!" Oberoi cried.

As Oberoi fell, Zelkovitz could see a small hole in his back. "You've been shot."

"I can't breathe," Oberoi said. "I'm going to die."

Like LaRuffa, Oberoi didn't die either. Ballistics evidence was inconclusive. But a Safeway employee reported seeing a dark-colored Chevrolet Caprice slowly leaving the parking lot after the shooting.

Then: September 15. Muhammad Rashid, thirty-two, was locking up Three Road Liquor in Brandy-wine, Maryland. The store was near LaRuffa's pizza place. The first two bullets missed Rashid's head. Then, a man shot him in the abdomen and took his wallet. Rashid didn't get a good look at him but said he had seen a big, dark car parked nearby. An ATF database showed that the bullet fragment came from the same .22-caliber gun used to shoot LaRuffa ten days earlier.

Next stop: September 21, Atlanta. At 12:15 A.M., Million A. Waldemariam was killed as he walked out of Sammy's Package Store. Waldemariam, forty-one, didn't work at the store but had been helping the owner. Waldemariam had noticed a suspicious car and went outside. He was fatally shot once in the head and in the back. His wallet had been taken. A .22-caliber bullet was recovered, but police were unable to link it to the two Maryland shootings, which might have alerted them to a shooter in a southbound dark sedan. The Georgia Bureau of Investigation doesn't put .22-caliber bullets into the ATF database. "The bullets are too small to get good results," said GBI spokesman John Bankhead. After Muhammad and Malvo were arrested, they were charged with that murder.

Next entry to the timeline: About nineteen hours after Waldemariam was shot, two women were shot as they closed a state-run liquor store in Montgomery, Alabama, one hundred and sixty miles to the south.

It happened around 7:30 that Saturday evening. Claudine Parker, fifty-two, and Kellie Adams, twenty-four, were locking up the Alabama Beverage Control Store close to Interstate 85. A man stepped from behind a red brick pillar and fired. The bullet hit Adams just below her skull and came out through her chin, leaving her badly scarred. Parker was shot in the back and killed.

Two officers across the street arrived moments later. A man standing over the women dropped a purse and ran. Officer Dwight Johnson, fresh out of the police academy, chased the man for a quarter of a mile. Then, an older model blue sedan cut him off for a minute. The suspect kept running, and Johnson finally lost him. Two witnesses chased a second man who dropped a gun catalog. Technicians later lifted a clean fingerprint from it. The handling of that print has been controversial. Some critics charge that if it had been run through national databases immediately, instead of just Alabama arrestees, Malvo and Muhammad might have been arrested sooner— before the October sniper shootings began.

Next on the timeline: September 23. At 6:40 P.M., Hong Im Ballenger was walking to her car after closing the beauty supply store she managed in Baton Rouge, Muhammad's hometown. She was shot in the head. Witnesses saw a large, blue car drive away from a field across from the parking lot. The black man driving the car picked up another man holding her purse and believed to be Malvo, according to arrest warrants. Police believe Muhammad fired the .223-caliber shot.

Next stop: September 28. An officer in Gulfport, Mississippi, noticed the Caprice in a parking lot, and ran a computer check of the New Jersey tags. They came back clean.

Four days later, the sniper shootings would begin in suburban Maryland.

* * *

In the days during and after the sniper siege, there was grumbling that the investigation wasn't proceeding smoothly. It's valuable to keep things in perspective. Often, it takes years to solve big, challenging cases where the perpetrators' identities are unknown. The sniper case, actually, was cracked remarkably quickly.

Still, since the arrests of John Muhammad and Lee Malvo, a number of police departments have tried to examine what worked and what didn't. The conclusion is that a lot of good police work and good cooperation occurred in the complex case. "But there is much improvement that needs to be made," Hanover County, Virginia, Sheriff Stuart Cook said. "Much of it has to do with the reluctance of some federal agencies to share information as rapidly as possible. We would get information quicker watching CNN news."

Another Virginia sheriff, Ronald Knight in Spotsylvania County, said he believes communication and coordination were commendable, considering the sprawling investigation. "There might have been some minor problems," he said. "But for the most part, it worked well when you considered the number of people on the case. Everyone rolled up their sleeves. There were no ego problems."

Prince William County, Virginia, Chief Charlie Deane said brass and street detectives exchanged information regularly. "Anytime you have an intense, flowing case like this, it is impossible to keep everyone up to speed, but this was a model of cooperation," he said. "It couldn't have been solved as quickly without the state and federal agencies."

To be sure, there were glitches, leaks and turf battles, but the ATF's Mike Bouchard said the law enforcement effort in the sniper case was unique. "I've never seen this number of departments come together before," Bouchard said. "Before nine-eleven, federal departments and local agencies only worked together halfheartedly. This is an example of how law enforcement will be done in the future."

Epilogue

In the days after John Muhammad and Lee Malvo were arrested at the rest stop on October 24, there was much jockeying to see which jurisdiction would be the first to try them. On November 8, U.S. Attorney General John Ashcroft stepped into the fray and announced that the men would be tried separately in Virginia. He said the venues were picked because they have the "best law, the best facts and the best range of available penalties." Virginia also has executed more people than any other state except Texas and is one of the few states that permit the execution of juveniles. Muhammad and Malvo have each been charged with capital murder, under a statute that makes it a capital offense to kill more than once within three years. They also have been charged with violating Virginia's new antiterrorism law that makes it a capital offense to intimidate the public and to coerce a government.

Lee Malvo has been charged in the October 14 shooting death of FBI analyst Linda Franklin at Home Depot and can be tried as an adult in Fairfax County in accordance with the January 15 ruling of Juvenile Court Judge Charles Maxwell. Minors can be executed in Virginia only if they are convicted of a capital offense in adult court. On January 22, a grand jury indicted Malvo on capital murder charges. On January 28, Fairfax County Circuit Judge Jane Roush set November 10 as the start of his trial. Fairfax's top prosecutor is Robert Horan. Malvo's lead defense attorney is Michael Arif, and Judge Roush appointed another lawyer, Craig Cooley, to work with Arif and other attorneys.

John Muhammad has been charged with the shooting death of Dean Meyers at the Sunoco station in neighboring Prince William County and is scheduled to face trial on October 14, 2003. He faces the death penalty if convicted of the capital murder charges. His scheduled trial date falls on the one-year anniversary of Linda Franklin's shooting. Prince William's top prosecutor is Paul B. Ebert. Muhammad's defense attorneys are Peter Greenspun and Jonathan Shapiro.

Altogether, Lee Malvo and John Muhammad have been accused of shooting thirteen people—ten fatally—during the October sniper attacks. They also have been either charged or are suspected of shooting nine other people, five fatally, from February through September 2002.

Technically, the other states that have filed charges against Muhammad and Malvo could seek to try them as well, even if the suspects are convicted in Virginia. But that raises the spectacle of prosecutors piling on convictions. Prosecutors in those states could forgo their right to try the pair and simply permit Virginia to be the state to punish them if they are convicted. Virginia law permits evidence from other states' cases to be introduced in the Virginia trials. "That is a chance for other folks' evidence to be aired in public, and it brings some closure," says Mark Corallo, a spokesman for the Justice Department. And that may suit some states just fine. As Montgomery, Alabama, Police Chief John Wilson says, "You can only put someone to death one time."

acknowledgments

This project would not have been possible without the vision and passion of Louise Burke, Mitchell Ivers and the supportive staff at Pocket Books and Esther Margolis at Newmarket Press. Their commitment and support have been unwavering throughout. Martin Krall, Peter Dwoskin, Kenneth Frydman and Ashley Gauthier all provided important legal and logistical expertise, without which this book could not have been produced. Janie Price, Lee Henry and John Artero weighed in with critical technical—and, occasionally, moral—support at key moments. Kate Forsyth provided timely, exhaustive and unfailingly creative research support for the project. Susan Vavrick's unsparing and incisive copyediting made the manuscript better in more ways than it is possible here to describe. *U.S. News* Design Director David Griffin's unerring eye was brought to bear on the project at the eleventh hour, and he made invaluable contributions. The magazine's director of photography, Bronwen Latimer, working with Senior Picture Editor Jenn Poggi, oversaw the careful selection and display of the photographs in the book.

This book would not have happened without the strong support of Brian Duffy, the editor of *U.S. News & World Report,* who made the storytelling vastly better. Thanks also to other editors at *U.S. News* who supported this project and our coverage of the sniper case: Gordon Witkin, Terry Atlas, Brian Kelly, Peter Cary, Susan Headden, Bruce B. Auster, Jodie Allen, Wray Herbert, Victoria Pope, Edward T. Pound, Jodi Schneider and Lisa Stein.

This book benefited from the outstanding reporting of the entire staff at *U.S. News,* but especially from Michael Schaffer, Samantha Levine, Noam Neusner, Katy Kelly, David E. Kaplan, Mark Mazzetti, Kenneth T. Walsh, Julian E. Barnes, Megan Barnett, Marianne Szegedy-Maszak, Jeff Glasser, Douglas Pasternak, Chitra Ragavan, Joellen Perry, Leonard Wiener, Matthew Benjamin, Anna Mulrine, Eli Sanders, Natalie Pompilio and Michael Reynolds. Our first-rate library staff provided invaluable research for our coverage, and our team of fact-checkers helped immensely. Our understanding of events also benefited from the fine work of the daily newspapers that covered this difficult story under tough deadlines: *The Washington Post, The New York Daily News, The New York Times, The Baltimore Sun, The Seattle Times* and *The Los Angeles Times.* Thanks for book-writing encouragement from historian James Tobin, agent Carol Mann and journalists Michael Tackett, Roger Simon and Wes Smith.

Thanks to Av and Lisa Goldstein for their assistance. Thanks to my family, especially Danny Goldstein, for being so patient.

And thanks, finally, to Mortimer B. Zuckerman, without whose unflagging support for the beyond-the-headlines reporting and vivid writing U.S. *News* delivers readers each week, this project could never have been attempted.